WORLD PEACE AND
WORLD GOVERNMENT
From Vision to Reality

J. Tyson has had an interest in world
government and international affairs ever
since he became a Bahá'í in 1970. He
studied Civil Engineering at Princeton
University and also took courses by
Richard Falk on international relations.
Among other jobs he has worked for the
Civil Defense Program in the United
States. His experience of the 'Third World'
comes from living in Liberia for four years
as a Bahá'í 'pioneer', and he has also
travelled in India. Since 1982 he has been
working at the Bahá'í World Centre in
Haifa.

A Bahá'í Approach

World Peace and World Government

FROM VISION TO REALITY

J. Tyson

GEORGE RONALD
OXFORD

GEORGE RONALD, Publisher
High Street, Kidlington, Oxford OX5 2DN
© J. TYSON 1986
All Rights Reserved

Reprinted 1986

British Library Cataloguing in Publication Data

Tyson, J.
World peace and world government : from vision to
reality : a Bahá'í approach.
1. International organization
I. Title
297'.891787   JC363

ISBN 0-85398-235-X

Printed in Great Britain by
Richard Clay Ltd, Bungay, Suffolk

CONTENTS

INTRODUCTION

The world's equilibrium hath been upset through the vibrating influence of this most great, this new World Order. Mankind's ordered life hath been revolutionized through the agency of this unique, this wondrous System – the like of which mortal eyes have never witnessed.[1]

There is no doubt that we live in an age of transition. The past years have witnessed change on an unprecedented and often frightening scale. Revolutions of thought and action have occurred in almost every field. Yet, one major area where there has been little real progress is in the field of international relations. The outmoded system of national sovereignty has not yet given way to a system of world order and world government. The elimination of prejudice, the equality of men and women, the need for universal education, the elimination of extremes of wealth and poverty, the establishment of a universal system of measurement – these and other Bahá'í ideals are accepted by a significant number of the general population as reasonable, progressive principles today. But the principle of the establishment of world peace through world government is still regarded by the vast majority as 'hopelessly idealistic' and 'much too far ahead of its time'.

Yet, Bahá'ís know that it is not ahead of its time. In a world tottering on the brink of self-destruction it is, in reality, long overdue. Therefore, it is essential that, in our proclamations and presentations about peace, we demonstrate that the much talked about issue of nuclear disarmament, as well as many of the other urgent economic and social problems of our times, are fundamentally linked to the curtailment of national sovereignty. World government must be shown to be not only a realistic solution, but indeed the *only* realistic solution to the global problems that threaten the life and the well-being of all mankind. Such a unified world is a stage of human development that we are destined to arrive at, if not by choice then by force of circumstance.

In this book we shall examine the reasons why world government is essential, the arguments commonly given against world government, and the compelling Bahá'í responses. We shall also look at some of the progress that has already occurred in this field and shall discuss some of the necessary steps and probable events leading to the establishment of a world government.

The creation of a world government is, in itself, only a small part of the process of establishing peacefulness between the diverse elements of mankind. This larger process requires the spiritual upliftment of humanity and the recognition of the oneness of mankind. It may well take several generations and will eventually lead to the establishment of what Bahá'u'lláh called 'the Most Great Peace'. Much can be found in the Bahá'í Writings concerning this larger aspect of peace, and Bahá'ís have been, and will be, in the forefront of promoting the unity it requires. The present work, however, focuses on a particular aspect of peace which is near at hand: the establishment of world government and what Bahá'ís call 'the Lesser Peace' – the ending of war among nations.

Introduction

As we enter the closing years of the twentieth century, we find ourselves on the threshold of the most significant event in mankind's secular history. The 'unity of nations . . . causing all the peoples of the world to regard themselves as citizens of one common fatherland', as spoken of by 'Abdu'l-Bahá in 1906, will occur, 'in this century'.[2]

The end of the century, which is also the end of a millennium, has symbolically represented 'the future' for several decades now. But as we enter the United Nations' Year of Peace (1986) the end of the century no longer seems to be the distant future but rather the near future – indeed the 'almost present'. It is no farther away from us in the future than 1972 is in the past. And so we are well-advised to be informed of, and ready for, this immeasurably significant change in the organization of human affairs. This is not to say that we, as Bahá'ís, will have a direct hand in organizing the world government. Shoghi Effendi, the Guardian of the Bahá'í Faith, states that the Lesser Peace is to be primarily established by the world at large.[3] But its birth has been a slow and painful one, beginning with World War I in 1914; and the diffusion of Bahá'í ideals will no doubt serve to hasten the process and bring it to a more perfect conclusion. The Guardian also said, in a letter written on his behalf in February 1932, 'There is no reason why the Bahá'ís should not take the lead in advocating such a Federation of the world, towards which the world is driven by forces it cannot control.'[4]

Chapter I

FROM 'DISARMAMENT' AND 'WORLD POVERTY' TO WORLD GOVERNMENT

As with many major problems, people often see symptoms without seeing the underlying causes. Millions of people feel threatened by nuclear arms and would like to see them eliminated. Others recognize (as Bahá'u'lláh certainly did) the horrible list of unmet human needs which results from spending large portions of national budgets on military expenses.

But in spite of the prolonged protests of millions of people of diverse economic, political and national backgrounds, the arms race has not been slowed down, much less halted or reversed. Indeed, we are asked to believe that the fact that the superpowers are even discussing the situation indicates 'progress'. But who can be satisfied as long as the policy of 'Mutual Assured Destruction' is the guiding theme of relations between nuclear powers, and the nuclear sword of Damocles hangs above our heads? Like a pair of feuding neighbors, the superpowers move along with pistols held to each other's heads, hoping that neither will twitch, go insane, or think for a moment that one can shoot and get away unharmed. Such is the state of the world at the close of the twentieth century.

Many people recognize that this situation is terribly

wrong, and are beginning to see that protest alone will not change it. Although recognition of the immediate problem is an important first step, it must be followed by a willingness to explore the deeper reasons which have prevented all disarmament efforts from becoming truly successful. Only after the problem is thoroughly understood can an effective solution be found.

We begin by exploring some of the concepts and relationships that form the basis for a proper understanding of this issue.

The Linkage between Disarmament and World Government

The first point that must be understood is that disarmament and world government are intrinsically linked together. This is because the very definition of sovereignty includes a nation's right to declare war. To eliminate that right (by effective disarmament) is to eliminate a major portion of national sovereignty. The vacuum thus created can only be filled by a true world authority. Nations would still be internally sovereign, but they could no longer force their way in the international arena.

Since disarmament is fundamentally linked to world government, all attempts to bring about disarmament without simultaneously establishing a world authority are destined to fail. Let us consider them briefly:

Unilateral disarmament is suggested by some people today. Although this idea seems to have some merit on the surface, its inadequacy is clear, as explained by 'Abdu'l-Bahá, the son of the Founder of the Bahá'í Faith:

No nation can follow a peace policy while its neighbor remains warlike . . . There is no justice in that. Nobody would dream of suggesting that the peace of the world could be brought about by any such line of action. It is to be brought about by a general and comprehensive international agreement, and in no other way . . .[1]

Bilateral nuclear disarmament to anything at or above 'deterrence levels', as is currently being discussed between the superpowers, is insignificant since, by definition, our mutual destruction would still be 'assured'. Who will find comfort in the knowledge that there are now 6,000 nuclear warheads pointed at his country, simply because the number was previously 10,000?

Disarmament below deterrence levels, in the absence of a world authority, would be de-stabilizing – causing nations to think that they might be able to attack without incurring much of a reprisal. While reducing the magnitude of a major war, it would greatly increase its likelihood.

To eliminate nuclear weapons altogether would invite a huge and even more expensive build-up in conventional forces. And again, it would be de-stabilizing, making war 'thinkable' once more. But more fundamentally, if a nation were losing a conventional war, no nuclear disarmament treaty would, in its hour of desperation, prevent it from re-building the nuclear weapons it needs. Further, without an organization to monitor continually the disarmament – which requires that it be given free access to all places on earth, both during and forever after the actual disarmament process – the treaty could easily be abused. On the other hand, if such an organization were created and given sufficient military and economic power to force the removal of nuclear weapons, it would in itself constitute a rudimentary form of world government.

Finally, elimination of all nuclear and conventional arms, without creating a world authority, would lead to complete anarchy – any small force would threaten everyone. This situation would be extremely unstable and would do almost nothing to increase our sense of security.

In practical terms, it can be stated that *governments will not move from a given state of security to a perceived state of less security*. One of their fundamental tasks is to provide security for their citizens. Yet, the world's trillion-dollar search for security through military power has led us to a state where we are less secure now than we were forty years ago. This is because the world has reached a state where security cannot be bought with greater armaments. It can only be achieved by replacing the system of international anarchy with a system of true international law. Any proposal that fails to take the lawlessness out of international relations fails to achieve greater security. And the only way to establish a system of true law between nations is to establish a functioning world government.

History supports the contention that meaningful disarmament cannot be achieved except in the context of a world authority: disarmament without an enforcement authority has already been tried and it proved to be a dismal failure. In signing the Kellogg-Briand Pact in 1928, sixty-three nations (representing nearly all of the world at that time) renounced war as an instrument of national policy and as a means of settling international disputes. But there was no authority to enforce the provisions of this agreement, and so it was easily broken, first by Japan in 1931 and then by Italy in 1935. It serves today as a reminder of the difference between a *treaty*, which falls apart as soon as any party to the treaty ceases to regard it as beneficial, and a governing *authority*, which maintains order in spite of disagreements between individual parties.

The Kellogg-Briand Pact also serves to illustrate a cause and effect error that is commonly found in discussing disarmament and peace: many people feel that disarmament treaties will cause true peace. In fact the reverse is true: true peace must be agreed to first. Disarmament will follow as its natural outcome.

Many writers in the field of international relations recognize the fundamental linkage between disarmament and world government. Certainly Grenville Clark and Louis Sohn recognized it when they wrote one of the most thorough and comprehensive plans for disarmament in 1958 entitled *World Peace through World Law*. In its introduction, Clark writes:

The proposition 'no peace without law' also embodies the conception that peace cannot be ensured by a continued arms race, nor by an indefinite 'balance of terror', nor by diplomatic maneuver, but only by universal and complete national disarmament together with the establishment of institutions corresponding in the world field to those which maintain law and order within local communities and nations.[2]

Emery Reves in *The Anatomy of Peace* put it quite simply: 'Collective security without collective sovereignty is meaningless . . . Only a legal order can bring security.'[3]

More recently, in his book *The Fate of the Earth*, Jonathan Schell has written:

9

If we are serious about nuclear disarmament – the minimum technical requirement for real safety from extinction – then we must accept conventional disarmament as well, and this means disarmament not just of nuclear powers but of all powers, for the present nuclear powers are hardly likely to throw away their conventional arms while non-nuclear powers hold on to theirs. But if we accept both nuclear and conventional disarmament, then we are speaking of revolutionizing the politics of the earth . . . We must lay down our arms, relinquish sovereignty, and found a political system for the peaceful settlement of international disputes.[4]

Albert Einstein, whose theory opened the door to the nuclear world, realized the implications of these weapons early on. His conclusion was the same. In September 1945 he wrote, 'At the present high level of industrialization and economic interdependence, it is unthinkable that we can achieve peace without a genuine supranational organization to govern international relations.'[5]

Jonathan Schell summarizes:

These statements, and countless others that might be quoted, form a remarkable consensus. One school favors world government and the other opposes it, yet they agree that if full nuclear disarmament (or total disarmament) is to be achieved world government is necessary. They make different choices, but they agree on what the choices are, and they agree that between the two there is no middle ground.[6]

Historically, war has been the final means of settling international disagreements. It cannot be eliminated without replacing it with some other means for settling disputes. World government, complete with world courts and a world force strong enough to enforce governmental decisions, is the only viable replacement for the war system. In the words of Shoghi Effendi:

Some form of a world Super-State must needs be evolved, in whose favor all the nations of the world will have willingly ceded every claim to make war, certain rights to impose taxation and all rights to maintain armaments, except for purposes of maintaining internal order within their respective dominions. Such a state will have to include within its orbit an International Executive adequate to enforce supreme and unchallengeable authority on every recalcitrant member of the commonwealth; a World Parliament whose members shall be elected by the people in their respective countries and whose election shall be confirmed by their respective governments; and a Supreme Tribunal whose judgment will have a binding effect even in such cases where the parties concerned did not voluntarily agree to submit their case to its consideration.[7]

World Government and a World Security Force

The linkage between world government and a world security force must also be clearly understood. However distasteful the idea may be to those who favor pure and total disarmament, the history of the UN has already demonstrated that the world authority will be largely ineffective unless it is given the real power necessary to enforce its decisions, to stop national re-armament and to hold the nations together when international disagreements arise. It need be only a relatively small force and relatively lightly armed, by today's standards, and should be drawn from, and scattered throughout, many countries of the world. It should be strong enough so that its combined forces could easily subdue the national guard and police forces of any country or group of countries, who themselves would only be lightly armed. The larger part of its membership would be reservists and most of its members could be drawn from small countries. It could also work in conjunction with the national guard forces of the various countries. Moreover, it would be called upon as a last resort, only after methods of mediation, arbitration and economic sanctions have failed.[8]

The General Assembly of the United Nations recognizes that real disarmament cannot be achieved without the simultaneous creation of an effective international peacekeeping force. The 'Program of Action' which resulted from their 1978 Special Session on Disarmament included the following statement:

Progress in disarmament should be accompanied by measures to strengthen institutions for maintaining peace and the settlement of international disputes by peaceful means. During and after the implementation of the programme of general and complete disarmament, there should be taken, in accordance with the principles of the Charter of the United Nations, the necessary measures to maintain international peace and security, including the obligation of States to place at the disposal of the United Nations agreed manpower necessary for an international peace force to be equipped with agreed types of armaments. Arrangements for the use of this force should ensure that the United Nations can effectively deter or suppress any threat or use of arms in violation of the purposes and principles of the United Nations.

General and complete disarmament under strict and effective international control shall permit States to have at their disposal only those non-nuclear forces, armaments, facilities and establishments as are agreed to be necessary to maintain internal order and protect the personal security of citizens and in order that States shall support and provide agreed manpower for a United Nations Peace Force.[9]

'Abdu'l-Bahá made it clear that the world government would need to have some means of enforcing its decisions when He said, '. . . there must be universal peace. To bring this about, a Supreme Tribunal must be established, representative of all governments and peoples . . . Should any government or people disobey [it], let the whole world arise against that government or people.'[10]

We cannot, at this stage of man's spiritual development, create a system that eliminates the use of force entirely, but we can create a system 'in which Force is made the servant of Justice' on an international scale.[11]

The Linkage between War and the Nation-State System

In addition to seeing the connection between disarmament and world government, and between world government and a world security force, it is necessary that people understand more fully the connection between war and the system of national sovereignty. In the words of Albert Einstein:

. . . the real cause of international conflicts is due to the existence of competing sovereign nations. Neither governments nor people seem to have learned anything from the experiences of the past and appear to be unable or unwilling to think the problem through. The conditions existing in the world today force the individual states, out of fear for their own security, to commit acts which inevitably produce war.[12]

The periodic occurrence of war can, therefore, be expected. Some people assume that in today's world, war occurs because of the clash between the communist world and the capitalist one, thinking that if only one group or the other would just go away, or give up, then all would be well. This is short-sighted. Carl-Friedrich von Weizsacker reminds us that:

The battle for world hegemony (whatever the 'world' was at that time) has been going on for thousands of years and, subjectively honest, the competitors have always seized on ideological means to brand the opponent as wicked, as barbarous, as representing a false system.[13]

Let us imagine for a moment that one of the present ideological systems was non-existent. Would this result in a complete and lasting peace? If all the capitalist and non-aligned countries disappeared, it is not hard to see that before long clashes and fighting would break out between the communist countries, many of which have their own separate version of communism. But the converse is also true: if the communist nations disappeared, the unity of the Western nations (much of which arises from having a common enemy) would also disappear. Economic competition would eventually lead to fear of dominance, mistrust, suspicion and protectionism, leading in turn to alliances, growth of armaments and, eventually, to war. Additional factors such as the relationship between over-production and joblessness, the armaments industry, and the tendency of the new generation to fail to comprehend the horror of wars experienced by previous generations, all combine to create a recognizable war–peace cycle over which the political ideologies of the day are simply a veneer.[14]

Thus, war is not only a 'right' of sovereign nations – it is also a regular and inevitable by-product of the nation-state system.

The Failure of Deterrence and Defense

Some people believe that a system of deterrence – the threat that an attack by one nation will bring about a devastating retaliation – is sufficient to prevent war. Thus nuclear weapons, in deterrence theory, are built solely to prevent their use. This system might at first seem workable, if the possibilities of human and machine error, sabotage, terrorism, the mental incapacity of a world leader and the possibility of one of the smaller nuclear nations upsetting the nuclear applecart, could be entirely ruled out. But the main reason that deterrence theory is not valid is because nuclear weapons are not 'created solely to prevent their use'. Their use has been considered, or threatened, during the Korean conflict, the Suez conflict, the Berlin crisis, the Cuban missile crisis, the Vietnamese war, the 1973 Arab-Israeli war, the invasion of Afghanistan and in at least one incident between the Soviet Union and China in 1969.[15] There are probably several others. In *The Fate of the Earth* Jonathan Schell puts it very poignantly:

For the fact is that the nuclear powers do *not*, as the statesmen so often proclaim, possess nuclear weapons with the sole aim of preventing their use and so keeping the peace; they possess them also to defend national interests and aspirations – indeed, to perpetuate the whole system of sovereign states. But now, instead of relying on war for this enforcement, as nations did in pre-nuclear times, they rely on the threat of extinction . . . For while the aim of survival causes statesmen to declare regularly that no purpose could ever be served by a holocaust, and that the aim of nuclear policy can only be to prevent such insanity, the pursuit of national objectives forces them to declare in the next breath that they are unwaveringly

15

resolved to perpetrate exactly this unjustifiable and insane action if some nation threatens a 'vital interest' of theirs.

Thus, the peril of extinction is the price that the world pays not for 'safety' or 'survival' but for its insistence on continuing to divide itself up into sovereign nations. Without this insistence, there would be no need to threaten annihilation in order to escape annihilation, and the world could escape annihilation by disarming as Russell, Einstein, and others recommended as early as the mid-nineteen-forties . . . [No] matter how one phrases it, the fact, which is rarely, if ever, mentioned either in the cold, abstract language of the theorists or in the ringing tones of the statesmen, is that the nuclear powers put a higher value on national sovereignty than they do on human survival, and that, while they would naturally prefer to have both, they are ultimately prepared to bring an end to mankind in their attempt to protect their own countries.[16]

Nor should it be imagined that the concept of deterrence is anything new.[17] Each major advance in weaponry has caused some people to feel that 'no one would dare attack us now' or 'peace will come because it would be too inhuman to use such destructive weapons'. Yet we have proved continuously that our ability to invent ever more deadly weapons is exceeded only by our willingness to use them.

There is the well-known case of the ruler who is fostering peace and tranquillity and at the same time devoting more energy than the warmongers to the accumulation of weapons and the building up of a larger army, on the grounds that peace and harmony can only be brought about by force. Peace is the pretext, and night and day they are all straining every nerve to pile up more weapons of war, and to pay for this their wretched people must sacrifice most of whatever they are able to earn by their sweat and toil. How many thousands have given up their work in useful industries and are laboring day and night to produce new and deadlier weapons which would spill out the blood of the race more copiously than before.[18]

This sounds as if it were written quite recently. In fact, it was written over a hundred years ago by 'Abdu'l-Bahá. 'Deterrence theory' is just an old idea, clothed in new words. It is no more a guarantee of peace today than it was several wars ago. The nuclear dimension may increase the length of the period of 'peace' between major wars, but the degree of destruction at the end of that period is even more greatly increased. '. . . and they think that they do well and that they are harbored in the citadel of security', wrote Bahá'u'lláh referring to mankind. 'The matter is not as they suppose: tomorrow they shall see what they now deny.'[19]

The nature of nuclear weapons makes it impossible to defend one's country against an attack in any meaningful way. The weapons can reach their targets more quickly than the time it takes for people to be notified and to reach an effective shelter. The major powers cannot begin to evacuate people beforehand because this would only cause the opposing nations to launch their weapons that much sooner. The effects of fire, the blast and the nuclear fallout are so intense and pervasive as to render any normal structure useless as a shelter. And the long term effects of such an attack would mean that large portions of the population would perish due to starvation, radiation sickness, disease and cold.

As to technological defenses, it should be noted that anti-ballistic missile systems were generally given up several years ago when it was recognized that they could be easily overcome by less expensive decoys. More recently, it has been suggested that orbiting laser beams might be capable of protecting us from nuclear missiles and bombers. But, aside from the extremely for-midable technical problems that stand in the way of producing such a device, no one seems to be addressing the question of preventing nuclear weapons from being smuggled piecemeal into a country, assembled and buried somewhere in each of the major cities. Or they could just as easily be 'delivered' to the waterfront of any coastal city by means of miniature submarines. The same people who previously devised the missile systems could surely devise several other alternative delivery systems. Fewer weapons would be needed since there would no longer be any need to destroy enemy missile sites – the lasers would have already rendered those missiles useless.

The point is simply this: where there is a will to deliver nuclear weapons, there is a way. Our problem is to eliminate the *desire* to deliver these weapons. An attempt to eliminate the *means* of delivery, in an age of ever-more sophisticated transport systems, is doomed to failure.

Communication, Transportation and the New Reality

Another basic concept that people fail to appreciate is the full implication of the revolution in transportation, communications and destructive potential that has occurred in the past 150 years. Although these represent just a part of the revolution of thought that created the modern world, they are a fundamentally important part.

Communication, Transportation and the New Reality

Eight major inventions, or groups of inventions, have appeared on the world scene in this age. Any one of them would alone have affected mankind's life in far-reaching ways. But taken together, they have had an even more profound and fundamental effect, inasmuch as they have shrunk the world's size (in terms of time-distances) and multiplied our knowledge of peoples and places all around the planet. And thus they have altered, in a very basic way, our concept of the world and changed the reality in which we live and move. The barriers of time and space that once separated mankind are now torn down. Hence, we are required to tear down the spiritual and emotional barriers that still separate us, in order to deal with this new reality.

The individual inventors could hardly have foreseen the total effect of their inventions: that these would cause so fundamental a change in mankind's perception of its world, removing us forever from the realm of independent nations and propelling us toward a new and unified world order. It is largely the failure of our institutions and our thought processes to keep pace with the changes implied by these inventions that has caused so much of the upheaval of our times.

I refer to these eight groups of inventions as the 'tele-mass' inventions because of their two common characteristics: they have affected the masses of mankind, and they have shortened the long distances that previously kept us separated into various states or tribes. They are:

1. The development of mass-printed newspapers, magazines and books, together with their distribution systems, which has created an international forum of ideas, educating and informing mankind, forcing upon us a consciousness of the

larger world, and an awareness of the condition of its peoples.

2. The development of radio and television, which has had an incalculable effect on mankind's awareness of his world, particularly because of the simultaneous growth of the accompanying radio and TV news organs. These inventions reach out to the literate and the illiterate alike and thereby encompass almost all of mankind. The portable radio in particular has the distinction of being the most universal of all modern inventions.

3. The telegraph, telephone, telex and the communications satellite have led to the establishment of a worldwide network of two-way communications, joining people together in thought easily, inexpensively and frequently, when physical meeting is not feasible. Information, which once moved at the speed of horse or sail, now flows at the speed of light.

4. The flow of materials and mass-produced products over the oceans has been profoundly affected, in terms of both volume and speed, by the invention of the modern ocean-going freighter. The volume of world trade that is made possible by this device is enormous. World trade has, in turn, created our world economy and our economic interdependence, which binds the world together more closely every day.

5. The ocean freighter, however, could not have created more than a world coastal economy were it not for the truck/train system that enables us to move large quantities of materials over large distances on land. Thus the world economic system affects everyone except those who do not live near a

road, railroad, port or navigable river. Few indeed
are unaffected!

6. The automobile/bus has done for man what the
truck/train system did for materials – making
possible rapid transportation of many people over
long distances. This has caused the intermixing of
peoples of diverse backgrounds on a day-to-day
basis, particularly in the urban centers, which in
turn has had a profound effect on man's thought and
his perception of himself. It has also shattered
certain social structures by enabling easy movement
to occur where little or none was possible before.

7. While the automobile has brought together states
and countries, the jet airplane has brought together
both countries and continents. The ability to hop
from country to country easily and inexpensively
has resulted in a surge in the number of world
travelers who are experiencing firsthand the
diversity of mankind. This has, perhaps more than
anything else, created our sense of living in a 'global
village'.

8. Finally, the nuclear weapon, coupled with the inter-
continental missile, although profoundly negative,
must also be included among the tele-mass inventions. While the other inventions have made world
unity possible, this invention makes it imperative. It
is forcing us to come to terms with each other, has
altered dramatically the very concept of war, and
may yet become the motive for our political union,
albeit out of fear rather than love.

The deeper result of these tele-mass inventions has
surrounded us slowly and quietly (with the exception of
the last one) and evermore thoroughly over the past 150

21

years. We now find ourselves in a drastically altered world. The distances between nations are gone. Like ice floes once free but now forced together in the ice-pack, the nations grind and chafe at each other's physical, economic and ideological borders. But the time must come when we bring ourselves into conformity with this new reality and unite our governments as we have already united our economic, information and transportation systems.

Bahá'ís recognize, of course, that it is not simply a coincidence that all of these technological advances have occurred in a single age. Rather, it is a result of the universal spiritual impulse that affects all of mankind whenever a new Manifestation of God appears. Bahá'u'lláh said, 'We have then called into being a new creation, as a token of Our grace unto men.'[20] Or again, 'Through that Word the realities of all created things were shaken, were divided, separated, scattered, combined and reunited, disclosing, in both the contingent world and the heavenly kingdom, entities of a new creation . . .'[21]

Nor, of course, are Bahá'ís alone in recognizing this fundamental change. In their book *Toward a Human World Order*, Gerald and Patricia Mische stated:

We are witnessing the final death throes of the principle of national self-sufficiency. The embryonic interdependencies that began to emerge 150 years ago with the Industrial Revolution are now in powerful bloom. Yet, at a time when national societies are mutually dependent on each other for goods and resources, political institutions continue to operate as if national self-sufficiency were still possible. The result is a multiplication of global and domestic crises as new wine remains in old skins.[22]

The new reality has been born. It will not go away.

Even if nuclear war were to destroy all our machines and our technical plans for building these machines, the very knowledge that they had been built before would ensure that they would be built again. Sooner or later, mankind would return to its present dilemma. Sooner or later, mankind will have to come to terms with this new reality.

In cycles gone by, though harmony was established, yet, owing to the absence of means, the unity of all mankind could not have been achieved. Continents remained widely divided, nay even among the peoples of one and the same continent association and interchange of thought were well nigh impossible. Consequently intercourse, understanding and unity amongst all the peoples and kindreds of the earth were unattainable. In this day, however, means of communication have multiplied, and the five continents of the earth have virtually merged into one. And for everyone it is now easy to travel to any land, to associate and exchange views with its peoples, and to become familiar, through publications, with the conditions, the religious beliefs and the thoughts of all men. In like manner all the members of the human family, whether peoples or governments, cities or villages, have become increasingly interdependent. For none is self-sufficiency any longer possible, inasmuch as political ties unite all peoples and nations, and the bonds of trade and industry, of agriculture and education, are being strengthened every day. Hence the unity of all mankind can in this day be achieved.[23]

Chapter II

THE WORLD GOVERNMENT DEBATE

The Case for World Government

If we intend to take the concept of world order and world government out of the realm of the visionary and into the realm of practical possibility, we must be able to answer the many questions that an ever-skeptical, often reluctant world is bound to put to us.

The first of these questions is, 'Why should we want a world government at all?' Although the answers may seem obvious to Bahá'ís, it is important not to assume that these answers are so readily apparent to others.

The elimination of the growing threat of extinction due to nuclear war should, of course, be reason enough. Studies on the effect of a full-scale nuclear war between the superpowers have shown that it could result in the extinction of man entirely, not so much because of the immediate effects but because of the longer-term ecological effects – the 'nuclear winter' caused by dust and smoke blotting out sunlight; and the destruction of the ozone layer in the upper atmosphere which would permit deadly ultraviolet radiation to reach the surface over an extended period of time.[1]

The magnitude of this reason is, of course, greater than that of any other. Most often people try to put the possibility of extinction out of their minds because it is such an 'unthinkable' thought. Since we cannot imagine what it would be like if a nuclear war were to occur, we imagine instead that it will not occur. This error in logic has been observed prior to revolutions and predicted natural disasters alike. It has been called 'a disbelief born of helplessness'. Alas, the refusal to investigate the seriousness of a problem has never caused the problem to go away.

But besides this major reason for world government, there are many other good reasons, which will be mentioned briefly. The problem of conventional/guerrilla warfare has hardly been reduced by the advent of nuclear weapons. Approximately sixteen million lives have been lost in 160 armed conflicts during the forty years of supposed 'peace' since the end of World War II.[2] It was, of course, the threat of conventional war, not the threat of nuclear annihilation, that motivated national leaders to take the first two steps toward establishing a world government, the creation of the League of Nations and the United Nations. The on-going conventional/guerrilla wars around the world provide constant demand for international government, although the apparent intensity of this demand varies according to where one happens to be living.

The incredible cost of maintaining and refining the military apparatus of the nation-state system, while crying human needs go unfulfilled, is a third reason for replacing that system with a world-state system. Over a hundred years ago Bahá'u'lláh wrote: 'O kings of the earth! We see you increasing every year your expenditures, and laying the burden thereof on your subjects. This, verily, is wholly and grossly unjust.'[3]

'Abdu'l-Bahá added:

The major part of the revenue of every country is expended over military preparations, infernal engines, the filling of arsenals with powder and shot, the construction of rapid-firing guns, the building of fortifications and soldiers' barracks and the annual maintenance of the army and navy. From the peasants upward every class of society is heavily taxed to feed this insatiable monster of war. The poor people have wrested from them all that they make with the sweat of their brows and the labor of their hands.

In reality war is continuous. The moral effect of the expenditures of these colossal sums of money for military purposes is just as deteriorating as the actual war and its train of dreadful carnage and horrors.[4]

Endless statistics are available. To quote just one:

As an indication of the unbelievable haemorrhaging of the world's resources into non-productive military budgets, just 7 months' worth of world military spending would be enough to pay for supplying clean water supplies and adequate sanitation for as many as 2 billion people (almost half the world's population) who now lack these bare essentials of health.[5]

Those who think that world government would be too expensive might consider the following statistic: 'The *entire* UN system could run for nearly two centuries on only one year's world military spending.'[6] (emphasis added)

Nor, it should be added, are the developing countries uninvolved in the armaments growth. The percentage of their Gross National Product which is devoted to military expenses has been growing consistently over the past two decades.[7] And this despite the fact that the basic needs of their people are the most critical in the whole world.

'Yet do we see your kings and rulers lavishing their treasures more freely on means for the destruction of the human race than on that which would conduce to the happiness of mankind.'[8] Bahá'u'lláh's statement to Prof. E. G. Browne in 1890 is certainly as true today as it was then, if not more so.

Apart from the avoidance of war and its costs, there is the simple fact that the world has already become one economic system. The problems of a world economic system cannot be resolved by a loosely knit group of national political systems. Whether the problem is balance of payments, international debt, fluctuating currency values, protectionism or insufficiency of resources, a world authority is required.

The interdependence of the peoples and nations of the earth, whatever the leaders of the divisive forces of the world may say or do, is already an accomplished fact. Its unity in the economic sphere is now understood and recognized. The welfare of the part means the welfare of the whole, and the distress of the part brings distress to the whole.[9]

World government is required for many other reasons – indeed too many to explore in detail here. But one can get an idea of the breadth of the need for world government simply by looking at a list of some of the agencies of the United Nations:

UN Environment Programme

World Food Programme

UN Fund for Population Activities

UN Conference on Trade and Development

UN Development Programme

UN Center for Human Settlements

UN Educational, Scientific and Cultural Organization

UN Children's Fund

General Agreement on Trade and Tariffs

International Monetary Fund

International Bank for Reconstruction and Development

Office of the UN High Commissioner for Refugees

Food and Agricultural Organization

World Health Organization

International Civil Aviation Organization

World Meteorological Organization

International Telecommunications Union

Universal Postal Union

Intergovernmental Maritime Organization

World Intellectual Property Organization

UN Industrial Development Organization

International Labor Organization

Publicity often focuses on the inability of the UN to deal adequately with international political problems and conflicts, while ignoring the tremendous benefits that have been brought about by these agencies. Each of them exists to solve problems which national governments are incapable of handling adequately. Each therefore represents a reason for world government. To whatever extent these organizations are incapable of fully discharging their duties, due to the restrictions of operating under a limited authority such as the United Nations, to that same extent do they cry out for a true, fully-empowered world government.

Responses to the Common Arguments against World Government

People have found a host of reasons for opposing the formation of a world government. If we are to change people's views on the subject, then in addition to demonstrating the positive need for world government, it is perhaps even more important for us to be able to demonstrate to them that their skepticism and fears are unfounded.

The very idea of world government has, alas, fallen out of fashion since the hope-filled days following the close of World War II, even though the need has grown ever greater since then. 'Realists' are skeptical, claiming that it is politically impossible to achieve the consensus, both between nations and within nations, necessary to create a world government, while 'idealists' may recognize that it is possible but, fearing Orwellian visions of oppressive, all-pervasive government, think that it is undesirable. Even the literature on the subject tends to speak of a 'world organization' or 'world law' or a 'world union' instead of 'world government' because of the skepticism and/or fear that the term sometimes engenders.

Most people, even if they haven't given the matter much thought, tend to respond in either, or both, of these negative ways. The fact that skepticism and fear have replaced hope and courage in so many hearts is a sad commentary on the spiritual condition of our age. Although a certain amount of doubt and caution is always warranted when approaching something unknown, the sort of automatic skepticism or fear that one often encounters when discussing the idea of world government is surely a part of the spiritual problem which we must overcome. We must challenge this skepticism and fear with well-reasoned arguments and with a positive attitude. To those who feel that 'It's just a dream', we must ask, 'Why?' We will thereby open the door to discussion of this most vital question of our time.

To the Skeptics

Skepticism Due to an Erroneous View of the Nature of Man

Much of the skepticism regarding the shift from national sovereignty to world sovereignty arises from man's negative view of himself and his capabilities. How often do those who advocate world peace receive the response that 'You can't change human nature!' Thus do they imply that war is a part of man's nature. But if humanity as a whole fails to recognize the spiritual nature of man, and if 'uncritical assent is given to the proposition that human beings are incorrigibly selfish and aggressive'[10] then man's hope of establishing a world without war is lost. If everyone were to regard themselves as no more than intelligent animals, and fighting as an intrinsic part of their nature, then, in this nuclear age, our 'mutual destruction' would indeed be 'assured'.

The Bahá'í teachings state that man has a higher, or spiritual, nature that can and should dominate his lower, or animal, nature. But lack of a spiritual education has often caused this good nature to remain hidden.

The Great Being saith: Regard man as a mine rich in gems of inestimable value. Education can, alone, cause it to reveal its treasures, and enable mankind to benefit therefrom.[11]

Past societies have faced and overcome other negative institutions that were supposedly a 'part of man's nature'. Slavery is probably the most obvious example of this. Man's spiritual nature, combined with the appropriate laws, has been, and will continue to be, capable of eliminating such negative elements of our life.

Thus, affirming and demonstrating that man's true nature is spiritual, and that he has the capacity to overcome the tendencies of his lower nature, is an essential part of the effort to establish world peace and a new world order. A detailed discussion of man's spiritual nature is beyond the scope of the present book, but one does not have to search far in the Bahá'í Writings to discover much material on the subject. (*Gleanings from the Writings of Bahá'u'lláh* and *Some Answered Questions* are some good starting points.)

Skepticism Due to an Erroneous View of History

If skepticism arises from an erroneous view of man's non-advancement on the individual level, it also arises from a similarly erroneous view of the history of man's social development. This skepticism is characterized by statements such as, 'Mankind has always divided itself into nations and it always will'. Although empires arose in a few places in our early history (and we tend to focus historical studies on these) much smaller units of social organization such as family groups, villages and tribes were the rule in ancient times, not the exception. A view of history seen in terms of ever-expanding units of organization is, in fact, much more accurate. Thus, the momentum of history carries us toward world organization rather than toward maintenance of the nation-state status quo.

Unification of the whole of mankind is the hall-mark of the stage which human society is now approaching. Unity of family, of tribe, of city-state, and nation have been successively attempted and fully established. World unity is the goal towards which a harassed humanity is striving. Nation-building has come to an end. The anarchy inherent in state sovereignty is moving towards a climax. A world, growing to maturity, must abandon this fetish, recognize the oneness and wholeness of human relationships, and establish once for all the machinery that can best incarnate this fundamental principle of its life.[12]

Indeed, the theme of the ending of the nation-state era is reflected in this century as we witness the ever more intense birth pangs of world civilization: World War I, leading to the League of Nations – our first feeble attempt at world government; World War II, leading to the more perfect but as yet unempowered United Nations; leading us now to the possibility of an even more deadly conflict which, if it occurs, will again invite the remaining portion of humanity to create a system of true world sovereignty.

Skepticism Due to the World's Size and its Diversity of Values

Another skeptical response is that the world is too big and too diverse to be united. But obviously, the first contention is not true. In terms of both travel-time and communications-time, the world today is much *smaller* than the thirteen American colonies were when they united in 1776. A hundred years ago people were surprised to learn that one could travel 'around the world in eighty days'. Nowadays one can easily travel around the world in eighty hours or less. If we wish to speak of missiles, the period is closer to eighty minutes. And in the case of world communications, it is essentially instantaneous. Truly, we are living in a 'global village'. The world is no longer too big for planetary management. It is, in fact, too small to do without it.

The problem of the world's diversity of values was once phrased like this: 'For a machinery of central justice to work satisfactorily, its judgments would have to be based upon a worldwide community of values. That community of values does not exist today.'[13] The first of these statements is partially true, but although international values are needed, they are required to operate on the international level only. Elsewhere, diversity in values can continue to exist. And agreement on values at the international level is not so difficult inasmuch as leaders and diplomats from all nations have, for many years, been participating in communal efforts. They are not strangers to each other.

The World Order Models Project[14] is often cited in this connection because it has dealt directly with the question of values. The project, which has been organized and run by a culturally diverse international group of scholars in the field of politics and international affairs, has recognized four main values which, it feels, can be accepted worldwide. These are: (1) Peace and non-violence; (2) Economic well-being; (3) Social justice; and (4) Ecological stability. Additional ones have also been proposed. Furthermore, considerable progress has been made at the UN in defining universal human rights. (The question of human rights is discussed in more detail in Chapter III below.) The point is that we are converging toward a sense of worldwide values. It is not beyond our reach.

Regarding the question of the size and diversity of the international organization, Shoghi Effendi has said:

To take but one instance. How confident were the assertions made in the days preceding the unification of the states of the North American continent regarding the insuperable barriers that stood in the way of their ultimate federation! Was it not widely and emphatically declared that the conflicting interests, the mutual distrust, the differences of government and habit that divided the states were such as no force, whether spiritual or temporal, could ever hope to harmonize or control? And yet how different were the conditions prevailing a hundred and fifty years ago from those that characterize present-day society! It would indeed be no exaggeration to say that the absence of those facilities which modern scientific progress has placed at the service of humanity in our time made of the problem of welding the American states into a single federation, similar though they were in certain traditions, a task infinitely more complex than that which confronts a divided humanity in its efforts to achieve the unification of all mankind.[15]

Skepticism Due to the Unwillingness of Leaders to Accept Significant Change

The skepticism that many people have about world government arises from the belief that world leaders are personally unwilling to give up their positions of power and submit to a world authority. Yet, when we investigate this we discover that many leaders, observing the world from their special vantage point, recognize the need for a world authority but fear that advocating this position would be politically impossible, as their constituency is not ready to accept such an idea. They are afraid of repeating Woodrow Wilson's mistake of trying to lead an unwilling people into the League of Nations and failing to find the necessary public support. Many of these leaders are part of an organization called the Parliamentarians for World Order, which includes over 600 members of legislatures from thirty-five countries. Also in the United States we find that:

. . . an encouraging number of Congressmen and women are already close to the movement for world order. Witness the organization called 'Members of Congress for Peace through Law' which has about 170 members. Although these legislators endorse the concept of world order, the present limited voter interest in world order results in a reluctance on their part to make it a practical priority in their personal political agendas.[16]

In 1973, in West Germany, the Chancellor Willy Brandt, said:

The Federal Republic of Germany has declared in its Constitution its willingness to transfer sovereign rights to supra-national organizations and it has placed international law above national law and made it directly applicable. This expresses the realization that the sovereignty of the individual and of nations can be secured only in larger communities, that the meaning and fulfillment of history can no longer be attributed to the nation-state . . .[17]

Similarly, Japanese leaders have stated in their Constitution that they 'forever renounce war as a sovereign right of a nation and the threat or use of force as means of settling international disputes.'[18]

As to the developing countries, they generally recognize that they have much more to gain than they have to lose by participation in a world government, just as they eagerly embrace participation in the United Nations. Since they are seldom listened to, in terms of the present superpower politics, a world order system that would give them a voice in the real management of planetary affairs is not likely to be rejected by them. Furthermore, any world organization which is dedicated to eliminating extreme international economic disparities is bound to be a source of great benefit to the developing nations and is likely to be welcomed by them.

It is not necessary that every national leader be willing to promote world government. 'Abdu'l-Bahá speaks of 'a certain number' of leaders who must 'arise, with firm resolve and clear vision, to establish the Cause of Universal Peace.'[19] If they are truly dedicated to the goal, their actions will allay the fears and suspicions of others, causing more and more leaders to accept the idea.

But at present we are faced with a curious paradox. People tend to believe that world government will not be formed because the leaders of the nations of the world aren't willing. Many of the leaders recognize the need for world government, but do not pursue it because they believe that the people aren't willing. The leaders are probably closer to the truth: the reluctance of people is a greater obstacle to world government than is the reluctance of their leaders, at least in the West. But people are reachable. Their views can be changed through education. The task rests largely with Bahá'ís and other world-minded individuals and organizations.

Skepticism Due to the Failure of the United Nations

Frequently, people respond to the idea of world government negatively by citing the failure of the United Nations to keep the peace, as it was intended to do. The response to this is clear: the UN was never given the authority it needed to keep the peace. The victorious nations, at the close of World War II, were not willing to cede enough of their national sovereignty to create an effective world body. As Donald Keys, co-founder of Planetary Citizens, explains:

. . . the United Nations was not designed to be all-powerful in international affairs; quite the contrary. The decisions of the General Assembly (where all States are members) are defined in the Charter as recommendations. However, what the Security Council decides is binding law under the Charter. The self-appointed Permanent Members (the Big Five: US, USSR, UK, France and China) of the Security Council, must agree (the Principle of Unanimity) for a proposal to be adopted. This is the origin of the 'veto' . . . Under these restrictions the UN was born a weakling – yet both the US and the USSR insisted on the 'veto' . . .

Nevertheless, the United Nations was a distinct improvement on the post World War I League of Nations, where the veto power was much more generally distributed. And, unlike the case of the League, which the United States refused to join, the US was a committed partner in the design of the UN from the beginning. Franklin Roosevelt did not want to see a replay of the repudiation of the League by Congress, remembering Woodrow Wilson's heartbreaking, futile effort to gain his country's support for the League.

Thus, while the League of Nations was admittedly too weak, the strength of the United Nations was intended to lie in peacekeeping by the Permanent Members – a built-in design for malfunction. This system fell apart almost immediately, and it has never been replaced by an adequate system for 'maintenance of international peace and security', which is the UN's 'prime directive'.[20]

In spite of its weaknesses, it is interesting to note that since the creation of the United Nations, traditional warfare, in the sense of one government blatantly attacking another with the aim of taking over its land, has become unacceptable by general consensus among the nations and is rarely seen today. This certainly represents a step forward.

Skepticism about the Transition

In addition, some are skeptical of the idea of world government because they simply cannot see the manner in which the transition will be made. This question of 'How do we get there from here?' is a very important one.

It is clear that if all the world's people wanted to establish a world government, it could be done. There are no technical obstacles that prevent it. It should also be clear that it would not even require the initial backing of all the world's people. If enough people of the democratic countries were solidly in favor of the idea, then there are several initiatives which these countries could take to demonstrate to the others that they sincerely want lasting peace and that they are willing to join with other nations in giving up certain aspects of their national sovereignty in favor of a world organization.

The first and largest step is one of education: teaching people that world government *is* achievable, and that its benefits far outweigh its costs. (Education and other aspects of the question of transition will be explored in greater detail in Chapter IV.)

Skeptics will sometimes claim that past transitions to larger social groupings have been achieved only when the group was threatened by a common external enemy. Today we, too, have a common enemy, but it is within us. It is our attachment to old forms of social organization, it is our fearfulness of each other, our prejudice, our greed, our thirst for power, and most of all, it is our willingness to destroy one another because of these things. Indeed, if our very existence were being threatened by violent creatures from another planet, we would certainly find a way to unite. But to admit that the enemy is within us takes a greater degree of spiritual maturity – a maturity that is, however, dawning upon us in this present century as the consciousness of the oneness of mankind spreads around the globe.

Bahá'ís are bound to find skepticism of all types as they promote the idea of world government. It is nothing new. 'Abdu'l-Bahá Himself was aware of this skepticism over a century ago, and warned us about it:

A few, unaware of the power latent in human endeavor, consider this matter as highly impracticable, nay even beyond the scope of man's utmost efforts. Such is not the case, however. On the contrary, thanks to the unfailing grace of God, the loving-kindness of His favored ones, the unrivaled endeavors of wise and capable souls, and the thoughts and ideas of the peerless leaders of this age, nothing whatsoever can be regarded as unattainable. Endeavor, ceaseless endeavor, is required. Nothing short of an indomitable determination can possibly achieve it. Many a cause which past ages have regarded as purely visionary, yet in this day has become most easy and practicable. Why should this most great and lofty Cause – the day-star of the firmament of true civilization and the cause of the glory, the advancement, the well-being and the success of all humanity – be regarded as impossible of achievement? Surely the day will come when its beauteous light shall shed illumination upon the assemblage of man.[21]

To the Fearful

People fear the idea of world government for a variety

of reasons. Their fears can usually be allayed, however, with the proper facts and reasoning.

Fear of the Unknown

A frequently encountered fear is the fear of the unknown or unprecedented, which is often implied without being outwardly expressed. We have created national governments before, but we have never created a world government. Fortunately, however, we are *not* without precedents. Federalism, the system in which several smaller regions are united under a trans-regional government, which has authority only over trans-regional affairs, is the system under which most large national governments and many smaller ones operate today. Argentina, Australia, Austria, Brazil, Burma, Canada, India, Mexico, Nigeria, Switzerland, the USA, the USSR, West Germany and Yugoslavia are included in this group. It is fair to say that the collective experience of mankind in creating federated systems is sufficient to assure us that a proper federated system for the world could also be created.

'Abdu'l-Bahá Himself endorsed the principle of federalism when He gave the following advice to a high official of the United States government:

You can best serve your country if you strive, in your capacity as a citizen of the world, to assist in the eventual application of the principle of federalism underlying the government of your own country to the relationships now existing between the peoples and nations of the world.[22]

The situation of the American colonies in particular has been recognized by many globally-oriented authors as being a valuable precedent because of its many parallels with today's world. Donald Keys writes:

We tend to forget that the United States as a potentially powerful Federal Republic was not the immediate and automatic result of the Revolutionary War, fought mainly for the independence of the thirteen colonies. The Revolutionary War ended in 1783, but the United States was not formed under its Constitution until 1789. In the interim, a loose assemblage of states existed under the Articles of Confederation. During those intervening years a change in consciousness took place: the thirteen states and their leaders became sufficiently 'nationalized' to permit formation of the new Union.

The thirteen former colonies at the war's end were highly autonomous, jealous of their sovereignty and prerogatives. Each state had its own government, its own army, and its own laws, including the laws regulating export and import of goods from the other states and travel of people among them. Trade barriers erected between the states became the source of intense friction, and it appeared that war might break out among the newly independent members of the Confederacy. Under tensions, pressures and frictions, smaller in scale but alike in kind to those which afflict international relations today, the original thirteen states had only one recourse: to become elements in a totally new organism, the United States of America. They took it, forming a federal union which allowed for the uniqueness of the members and combined their energy, vision, power and commerce. The Constitution became the supreme law of the land in matters not reserved to the states.[23]

The life-or-death importance of unity was recognized in those days, and was expressed in the phrase 'Unite or Die!' – a phrase which also seems highly applicable to the situation in which the world finds itself today.

It might also be instructive to look at another group of roughly fifty states which have a colonial past, for comparison. As the continent of Africa was emerging from colonialism, the idea of establishing a pan-African government was advocated by some of the new leaders. If this had been done, and if a broadly based pan-African force had been created that would protect the governments of each country, while guaranteeing the rights of the individuals within those countries, then countless revolutions and coups d'état and much bloodshed would have been avoided. In the resulting atmosphere of stability, economic development would have flourished. Although a certain amount of money would have been required to run the pan-African government, far more would have been saved on armies and armaments, and would now be available to help improve the lives of millions of people in this desperate part of the world. Conversely, one can well imagine the many wars that would have by now occurred both between and within the American states if the thirteen colonies had chosen to remain separate in 1789. The choice between world unity and world disunity is not unprecedented. In these two regional examples we see the stark results of the difference between working together under one order, and trying to work separately under several conflicting governments.

The Fear of Uniformity and Over-Centralization

The fear of forced uniformity and over-centralization are certainly among the fears that are most often voiced. If one does not happen to like the standard world system, culture or economy, where would one go to find an alternative? To this we must answer that there is no need to alter the diversity among nations and cultures. The principle of unity in diversity is one which the Bahá'ís consider essential. The choice of federalism, with its emphasis on decentralization and the freedom of member states to control their own internal affairs, is consistent with this principle. The great cultural diversity of the Bahá'í world, which not only is allowed to exist but is actively encouraged, is evidence of our devotion to the concept of unity in diversity. Bahá'u'lláh's teaching regarding the establishment of a universal auxiliary language to facilitate understanding without eliminating native languages, so essential to cultures, is further evidence. Finally, we should turn again to the words of the Guardian:

[The purpose of the world-wide Law of Bahá'u'lláh] is neither to stifle the flame of a sane and intelligent patriotism in men's hearts, nor to abolish the system of national autonomy so essential if the evils of excessive centralization are to be avoided. It does not ignore, nor does it attempt to suppress, the diversity of ethnical origins, of climate, of history, of language and tradition, of thought and habit, that differentiate the peoples and nations of the world. It calls for a wider loyalty, for a larger aspiration than any that has animated the human race. It insists upon the subordination of national impulses and interests to the imperative claims of a unified world. It repudiates excessive centralization on the one hand, and disclaims all attempts at uniformity on the other. Its watchword is unity in diversity . . .[24]

The principle of unity in diversity is recognized by most of the world order writers. One example of this is the *Constitution for the Federation of Earth*, produced by the World Constitution and Parliament Association, which in its preamble cites the principle of unity in diversity as 'the basis for a new age when war shall be outlawed and peace prevail'.

The principle of unity in diversity extends even into the realm of national political systems, which could exist in harmony under one world authority. In a talk given in New York, 'Abdu'l-Bahá answered the question 'Is it not a fact that universal peace cannot be accomplished until there is political democracy in all the countries of the world?' by saying:

It is very evident that in the future there shall be no centralization in the countries of the world, be they constitutional in government, republican or democratic in form . . . [E]ach province will be independent in itself, but there will be federal union protecting the interests of the various independent states. It may not be a republican or a democratic form. To cast aside centralization which promotes despotism is the exigency of the time. This will be productive of international peace.[25]

National economic systems, as well as political systems and cultures, could be diverse. Nations could still choose the economic system that best suits their local needs and cultural background. On the global level, the establishment of a universal currency, a world central bank, a system of world taxation and a world development authority would do much to balance monetary flows between countries and thus to eliminate most of the problems that currently arise from monetary imbalances. Such a system would encourage economic development, particularly in the less developed areas of the world, and the relaxation of trade barriers. Moreover, the elimination of military budgets would liberate an immense amount of resources and labor, which could then be devoted to constructive purposes. While each nation could choose both its own preferred internal economic system and the degree to which it wished to participate in the world economy, national leaders could work together with international authorities to coordinate their economic plans in a coherent international framework. This would take much of the uncertainty and many of the erratic tendencies out of international financial affairs.

Fear of the Loss of Freedom

Another fear of world government is that it will be the cause of the loss of freedom on both the individual and national levels. Unquestionably, it will mean the loss of a nation's freedom to do whatever it wishes in the international realm, as the rule of law replaces the rule of force. But a proper federal constitution will strictly limit the powers of the world government to those pertaining to the international realm only. All other questions will be resolved at the national or local levels. On these levels, nations will see an *increase* in their freedom and ability to assist their people to develop and prosper. The nation-state system has given nations an illusion of freedom, while in fact creating many economic and military constraints. For instance, is a nation 'free' to devote its energy to improving the life of its people, when a neighboring nation is busily producing weapons? Obviously, it is not.

As to the question of individual freedom, the world federal government would need to establish a basic universal code of human rights, guaranteed in all nations. The existing nationally-guaranteed rights of individuals would not be diminished, except for the occasional cases where they lead to the infringement of another's rights. It may be necessary to bring the code into force in a gradual manner so that its effect would not be disruptive. (We will return to the question of human rights in Chapter III below.)

Fear of the Tyranny of Groups of States

The 'tyranny of minor states' is one of the most frequently heard objections to the UN's General Assembly, and any other such world body that is based on the one-nation-one-vote system. Certainly, 51% of the nations can represent much less than 51% of the world's people. The Bahá'í response to this is clear and simple. 'Abdu'l-Bahá said, 'The number of these representatives should be in proportion to the number of inhabitants of that country.'[26] Thus, the one-nation-one-vote system is not acceptable.

The smaller states will no doubt complain that more than half of the world's population resides in four countries – China, India, the USSR and the USA – and that these four nations, working together, could effectively control a world legislature, thus creating a 'tyranny of the majority'. There are several possible ways of resolving this problem. In the American precedent, the problem was resolved by creating two houses of legislature, one in which states were represented equally and one in which states were represented by population. This is workable, if somewhat unwieldy.

A variant on this approach, taken by the World Constitution and Parliament Association, is to add a third 'House of Counsellors', nominated by the colleges and universities of the world. Laws would be adopted by passage in any two out of the three houses. This prevents any one house from having what amounts to a veto power, and thus makes the system less unwieldy and more responsive to change.[27]

In His Tablet to the Hague,[28] 'Abdu'l-Bahá suggested that a single group of representatives should be selected who would represent both their people and their country. A single chamber parliament would avoid the cumbersome aspects of a multi-cameral system. The representatives would be indirectly elected by the people of each country (i.e. the representative portion of the national governments would elect the representatives to the world legislature). These would then be confirmed by the rest of the government (the upper chamber, the president, and/or the cabinet, as the case may be) so that they would represent both the people and the government of their country. The members of this world legislature would elect, from among their number, the most eminent to serve on the Supreme Tribunal, the judicial branch of this world government. (This may have been intended to be only *one* formulation that is compatible with the Bahá'í teachings, not *the only* formulation compatible with them. Regarding the Supreme Tribunal, for instance, the Guardian stated that it 'is an aspect of a world superstate; the exact nature of its relationship to that state we cannot at present foresee.'[29])

While countries with greater populations would indeed have more votes in the legislature, no country would ever have more than half of the world's population, due to physical limits alone. Given the great diversity between these nations, it seems highly unlikely that they would reconcile their views merely for the sake of collaborating against the smaller states. Furthermore, if each member of the legislature acted primarily as a representative from his particular section of his country, instead of as a member of a national delegation, the representatives from a single country would often vote differently on a given issue, depending on the requirements of their particular locality. In addition, if politics were re-organized so that all of the representatives were pledged to vote, as world citizens, for whatever they determined to be best for the world as a whole, then many of the political alignments and fears of tyranny would disappear.

But most importantly, the rights of all nations would be clearly delineated in the constitution and carefully protected by the world court so that no 'tyranny' of any group of nations – minority, majority or otherwise – could exist.

Fear of Large Organizations

The complaint that world government would become too large is yet another fear that is often voiced:

The real problem with world government . . . is not that it is 'impossible', or 'utopian' – for if enough people want it they can surely have it – but that if we choose it we get more than we want. The heart sinks at the thought of world government not because it is 'unrealistic' but because it is all too real . . . We want relief from the nuclear peril, but if we sign up for world government as the means of getting it we find that global institution after global institution is inexorably delivered on our doorstep thereafter, each one equipped to meddle in some new area of our lives.[30]

To this we must first answer that the whole purpose of federalism is to preserve as much local autonomy as possible and to limit the tendency for the central government to expand beyond the boundaries of regulating essential international affairs. We are surely conscious that 'the evils of excessive centralization', as mentioned above, must be avoided.

Nevertheless, it must be acknowledged that there are many areas which require international regulation, and

48

therefore the world government will seem to be fairly big. Indeed, the necessity of regulating many areas of international affairs is but a testimony to the great need for world government and to the fact that it is long overdue. If a world government had been established in the early 1800s, its role initially would have been rather limited and it would have expanded slowly according to the needs of the times. But we have postponed the task of creating the international body for a century and a half, so of course we have a tremendous amount of catching-up to do, and the number of organs required for the world government appears to be many. But we cannot allow our past failure to act on this issue to become an excuse for further failure to act.

Another way of looking at this is to recognize that war has been used as the ultimate solution to *all* international disagreements, regardless of their nature. If we propose to substitute world government for the war system, then it too must be capable of resolving *all* types of international disagreements. Thus, it requires several branches and organs.

We must also point out that the creation of a world government will enable national governments to reduce their size. It will be not only possible to dismantle most of the military aspects of the national government, but to dismantle other structures of national government which have been trying (often in vain) to deal with any of the several international problems that currently plague them. Freed from the fear of the economic or military domination of their neighbors, and from the responsibility of having to solve every international problem, the over-bloated size of many national governments could be reduced to more reasonable levels.

Fear of Bureaucracy

Allied to the fear of large, intrusive government is the fear that the world government will become a big bureaucracy, incapable of dealing with any issue efficiently. This bureaucracy can be avoided, to a certain extent, by carefully organizing the various branches of government in such a way as to promote action rather than inaction, flexibility rather than rigidity. Wherever possible, its specialized agencies could be given a high degree of autonomy, similar to the UN's specialized agencies, thus promoting a more decentralized, responsive and creative organization.

Bureaucracy can also be avoided, at least in part, by the establishment of an office whose duty is to assist individuals in dealing with such a large organization, to monitor the development of the organization and to make proposals for changing it, thus enabling world government to be a dynamic, efficient and organic body. Such an office has been proposed in *A Constitution for the Federation of Earth* under the title of 'world ombudsman'. We will return to this later.

But much of the problem of bureaucracy is found at the level of the individual worker. If the civil servant is capable, if he is devoted to serving mankind rather than serving himself, if he is guided by overall goals rather than the minute details of policies, if he accepts the organizational changes that necessarily arise from the changing needs of the times rather than jealously guarding his particular domain, if he is willing to follow the principles of consultation rather than acting in a dictatorial manner, then his organization will have avoided most of the problems of modern bureaucracies. The problem of bureaucracy in any large organization is primarily a spiritual problem. The Bahá'í teachings have much to offer in this regard.[31] They will no doubt be incorporated into large organizations to an ever-greater degree in the period between the establishment of the Lesser Peace and the coming of the Most Great Peace, as envisaged by Bahá'u'lláh.

Fear of a Dictatorship

An additional fear that is often expressed, which is perhaps the gravest of all, is the fear that the world government could be corrupted into some form of dictatorship, empire or totalitarian state from which there would be no escape. These fears are fed by several 'anti-utopian' novels which have appeared, portraying an omnipresent, dictatorial government which totally overwhelms and crushes the human spirit.

In response to this we should note, as was stated above, that there *are* precedents for the creation of a world government. The process of establishing a federated government, guided by the will of the majority, prevented from transgressing into the domain of non-federal affairs, protecting individual rights, and having sufficient checks and balances to prevent the concentration of too much power in any one individual or group of individuals, is not unknown to mankind. The size of the territory over which it governs may be new, but the pattern is not. Indeed, by broadening the basis of federal government to include the whole world, the prospects of preserving its integrity are increased, not diminished. Once a constitution is created and promulgated throughout the world and has received the support of the masses of mankind, it is impossible to imagine how any group could be big enough, widespread enough, powerful enough and yet secret enough successfully to subvert such a broadly founded government.

It should also be made clear that the threat of the establishment of a world dictatorship or a world empire, comes more from maintaining the present system than from adopting a federated world government. This is because the present system is likely to lead us into a major war, after which people will be willing to follow anyone who promises them order and security. Such a situation is fertile ground for creating future dictators. It is unquestionably better to create a well-planned world government rather than to hold back and wait until an unplanned world dictatorship is forced upon us.

Skepticism and Fear Caused by Religious Beliefs

Some religious people will claim that the creation of a world government is insufficient to solve all the problems of humanity because a world government cannot address the spiritual element of the problem. Bahá'ís would wholeheartedly agree with such a view. The spiritual development of mankind is the ultimate solution to problems induced by materialism. In the words of Bahá'u'lláh: 'The corrosion of ungodliness is eating into the vitals of human society; what else but the Elixir of His potent Revelation can cleanse and revive it?'[32]

In the same vein, the Guardian wrote:

Not even, I venture to assert, would the very act of devising the machinery required for the political and economic unification of the world . . . provide *in itself* the antidote against the poison that is steadily undermining the vigor of organized peoples and nations.[33] [emphasis added]

Thus, world government is not seen as a panacea for all of the world's ills, but rather as a necessary first step to resolving them. Although the resulting peace will be the greatest peace the world has yet known, it is still referred to as the 'Lesser' Peace because there will still be numerous problems which stem from materialistic attitudes. But the abolition of war will do more than eliminate the threat to human survival and save untold resources. It will also eliminate the source of much of the fear, suspicion, and hatred that now plagues mankind. Thus it will 'bring in its wake the spiritualization of the masses.'[34] When man eventually reaches the point where the motive for peace is no longer fear of mutual destruction but genuine love for one's fellow man, and when the philosophy of materialism gives way to the universal recognition of one God, then the 'Most Great Peace', the Kingdom of God on earth, will have begun.

Some people of Judeo-Christian background will no doubt assert that world peace cannot be established until the Messiah comes. Again, Bahá'ís are in full agreement. In this case, the task of promoting the idea of world government is a matter of demonstrating that the Promised One of Judaism, Christianity and all other religions, has already come, and that He has given mankind both a plan for establishing world peace and the spiritual and material means to implement it.

Occasionally, one will also find people who have fears of world government because of their understanding of certain passages of prophecy in the Bible. The question of Biblical interpretation is a very large topic and an adequate discussion of it is beyond the scope of this book. However, a few points should be explained and sources of further information cited.

The source of these fears can usually be found in the second half of Daniel and in the second half of the book of Revelation which refer to an evil 'fourth kingdom' and to 'the beast' which will lead it. Some Christians may suggest that this refers to a world government. Upon closer inspection, however, it becomes clear that such suggestions fail to fit the present situation. Christian authors themselves state that this 'kingdom' is to be a confederation of ten kings from countries that were once part of the old Roman Empire.[35] Clearly, a government which incorporates *all* of the nations of the world, including the most powerful ones which are *outside* the boundaries of the old Roman Empire, is an entirely different thing.

Since Bahá'ís accept the Divine origin of all religions, we are able to see how prophecies span the ages and link together these different religions. From this much broader perspective, we can see that many of the prophecies of the past religions have already been fulfilled, but usually not in the manner that religious leaders expected. Christians will certainly acknowledge that a similar situation existed after the coming of Jesus: many of the Old Testament prophecies were fulfilled by His coming, but not in the manner that the Jewish religious leaders had anticipated. Furthermore, the fact that the Wise Men of the East were Zoroastrians, who successfully used Zoroastrian religious prophecy to foresee the birth of Jesus, serves as an example of how such prophecy forms a link between religions that outwardly appear to be different.

In the case of the Biblical prophecies in question,

'Abdu'l-Bahá explains that they relate to the Islamic period and to the corruption of the larger branch of Islam under the Umayyad dynasty and the Caliphs, who ruled over most of the land that had once belonged to the old Roman Empire.[36]

Bahá'ís could also direct people's attention toward the less cryptic prophecies of Isaiah, which clearly indicated the future establishment of peace and a world government of justice:

He shall judge between the nations, and shall decide for many peoples; and they shall beat their swords into ploughshares, and their spears into pruning hooks; nation shall not lift up sword against nation, neither shall they learn war any more.[37]

For to us a child is born, to us a son is given; and the government will be upon his shoulder, and his name will be called 'Wonderful Counsellor, Mighty God, Everlasting Father, Prince of Peace'. *Of the increase of his government and of peace there will be no end*, upon the throne of David, and over his kingdom, to establish it, and to uphold it with justice and with righteousness from this time forth and forevermore.[38] (emphasis added)

In sum, we can see that although many arguments are given as to why mankind cannot, or should not, create a world government, none of them are truly valid. In order to move the concept of a new world order from vision to reality, the subject must be raised, the questions must be faced and the answers clearly given. And this must be done repeatedly, until the vision becomes the possible, the possible becomes the probable, and the probable becomes incarnated in a living world organization.

Chapter III

VISIONS OF THE NEW WORLD ORDER: BAHÁ'Í AND OTHER CONTRIBUTIONS

The first step toward creating the new world order is to envisage its outline in our minds. Several outlines have already been proposed, some of which are described below.

Bahá'í Proposals for the Lesser Peace

Many of the Bahá'í proposals have already been mentioned. To complete this description, the following quotations are given.

Concerning the need to hold some form of a constitutional convention, and to establish the principle of collective security, Bahá'u'lláh has said:

The time must come when the imperative necessity for the holding of a vast, an all-embracing assemblage of men will be universally realized. The rulers and kings of the earth must needs attend it, and, participating in its deliberations, must consider such ways and means as will lay the foundations of the world's Great Peace amongst men. Such a peace demandeth that the Great Powers should resolve, for the sake of the tranquillity of the peoples of the earth, to be fully reconciled among themselves. Should any king take up arms against another, all should unitedly arise and prevent him. If this be done, the nations of the world will no longer require any armaments, except for the purpose of preserving the security of their realms and of maintaining internal order within their territories.[1]

'Abdu'l-Bahá further elucidates this theme and describes four requirements of a universal peace covenant:

They must make the Cause of Peace the object of general consultation, and seek by every means in their power to establish a Union of the nations of the world. They must conclude a binding treaty and establish a covenant, the provisions of which shall be sound, inviolable and definite. They must proclaim it to all the world and obtain for it the sanction of all the human race . . . In this all-embracing Pact the limits and frontiers of each and every nation should be clearly fixed, the principles underlying the relations of governments towards one another definitely laid down, and all international agreements and obligations ascertained. In like manner, the size of the armaments of every government should be strictly limited, for if the preparations for war and the military forces of any nation should be allowed to increase, they will arouse the suspicions of the others.[2]

'Abdu'l-Bahá also speaks of the organization necessary to maintain this Pact, in terms of a 'Parliament of Man' and a 'Supreme Tribunal'.[3]

In addition to Shoghi Effendi's description of the future world order quoted in the first chapter of this book, he has given us the following glimpse of our future world, some aspects of which will constitute the beginning of the Lesser Peace:

The unity of the human race, as envisaged by Bahá'u'lláh, implies the establishment of a world commonwealth in which all nations, races, creeds and classes are closely and permanently united, and in which the autonomy of its state members and the personal freedom and initiative of the individuals that compose them are definitely and completely safeguarded. This commonwealth must, as far as we can visualize it, consist of a world legislature, whose members will, as the trustees of the whole of mankind, ultimately control the entire resources of all the component nations, and will enact such laws as shall be required to regulate the life, satisfy the needs and adjust the relationships of all races and peoples. A world executive, backed by an international Force, will carry out the decisions arrived at, and apply the laws enacted by, this world legislature, and will safeguard the organic unity of the whole commonwealth. A world tribunal will adjudicate and deliver its compulsory and final verdict in all and any disputes that may arise between the various elements constituting this universal system. A mechanism of world inter-communication will be devised, embracing the whole planet, freed from national hindrances and restrictions, and functioning with marvellous swiftness and perfect regularity. A world metropolis will act as the nerve center of a world civilization, the focus towards which the unifying forces of life will converge and from which its energizing influences will radiate. A world language will either be invented or chosen from among the existing languages and will be taught in the schools of all the federated nations as an auxiliary to their mother tongue. A world script, a world literature, a uniform and universal system of currency, of weights and measures, will simplify and facilitate intercourse and understanding among the nations and races of mankind. In such a world society, science and religion, the two most potent forces in human life, will be reconciled, will cooperate, and will harmoniously develop. The press will, under such a system, while giving full scope to the expression of the diversified views and convictions of mankind, cease to be mischievously manipulated by vested interests, whether private or public, and will be liberated from the influence of contending governments and peoples. The economic resources of the world will be organized, its sources of raw materials will be tapped and fully utilized, its markets will be coordinated and developed, and the distribution of its products will be equitably regulated.

National rivalries, hatreds, and intrigues will cease, and racial animosity and prejudice will be replaced by racial amity, understanding and cooperation. The causes of religious strife will be permanently removed, economic barriers and restrictions will be completely abolished, and the inordinate distinction between classes will be obliterated. Destitution on the one hand, and gross accumulation of ownership on the other, will disappear. The enormous energy dissipated and wasted on war, whether economic or political, will be consecrated to such ends as will extend the range of human inventions and technical development, to the increase of the productivity of mankind, to the extermination of disease, to the extension of scientific research, to the raising of the standard of physical health, to the sharpening and refinement of the human brain, to the exploitation of the unused and unsuspected resources of the planet, to the prolongation of human life, and to the furtherance of any other agency that can stimulate the intellectual, the moral, and spiritual life of the entire human race.[4]

Clearly, not all of these things will be achieved at the same time. Some, such as the system of world inter-communication and the universal system of weights and measures, are already largely in place. Others will develop during the period of the Lesser Peace, while still others will not occur until the period of the Most Great Peace, when the vast majority of the world's people recognize Bahá'u'lláh, which may be many decades, or a few centuries, away.

The Lesser Peace is much nearer to us. Its initiation would seem to require, as a bare minimum, the establishment of a true world legislature or parliament, a binding world tribunal or court, a world executive and an effective international force, together with universal disarmament – both nuclear and conventional – the creation of a code of the rights of individuals and nations, and some form of international taxation.[5] As previously stated, Bahá'ís do not regard these as a panacea for all the world's ills, but rather as the first necessary step, without which the other major problems that currently plague mankind will remain unresolved.

One important feature of the Bahá'í model is its emphasis on unity instead of divisiveness. This has several implications, one of which is that all members of the world government must be dedicated to promoting the 'good of the whole' rather than the short-term advantage of any part of mankind. They should regard themselves as world citizens and as the loving parents of all mankind, not as jealous neighbors. This implies a profound change in the concept of representative government, for the representatives would not automatically promote whatever seems best for their constituency, nor could they campaign on such a basis. They would serve the legislature primarily in their capacity as experts of their local district, capable of providing detailed information about local views, needs and conditions. As such, they would bring an enormous amount of knowledge to bear upon world problems. But they would be obliged to vote according to whatever they find to be best for the whole of mankind, not according to the dictates of their constituency.

Devotion to serving the whole of mankind would also preclude the possibility of world political parties, for one cannot be truly dedicated to the best interests of both a party and to mankind as a whole. This would mean that politics on the world level would be considerably different from politics as it is practiced in most nations today (although some Third World countries may find the concept of entrusting their affairs to the 'wisest elders' as being not far removed from their own cultural traditions). By excluding party politics, we also exclude much of the unhealthy concentration of power in the hands of a few. This would do much to alleviate fears that any one group would come to dominate the world legislature. By eliminating the possibilities of individual power and its rewards, the task of working for the world government will attract those who truly wish to serve humanity and not those who crave power.

The process of nomination and elections would be considerably different – several possibilities could be suggested. (See the comments under 'Fear of the Tyranny of Groups of States' for 'Abdu'l-Bahá's specific suggestions.) The basis for judgment between various candidates would be their qualifications based on their education, experience and dedication to serving humanity.

Under such a system, legislative consensus is reached by consultation rather than by the give and take of power politics. The Bahá'í concept of consultation aims to combine the knowledge and problem-solving capacity of several minds, with the least possible amount of internal friction between individuals. It is far removed from the various sorts of power politics that result in disunity within most nations today.

Bahá'ís have put these principles into practice in their own administrative organization and have demonstrated that they are not only workable but that, once the requisite skills are learned, they are highly effective.

Most of the non-Bahá'í ideas for world government are largely extrapolations from models of government that are culturally Western. The Bahá'í model includes the best aspects of the Western model, but introduces new themes of its own, outlined above, based on its concept of unity. These themes may seem strange to some at first. However, anyone who observes the problems that plague existing national governments as a result of their internal disunity will readily acknowledge the value of these unifying proposals.

The Bahá'í Faith is not alone, of course, in setting forth ideas on world government. There are several detailed proposals, at least three of which are largely in line with the Bahá'í expectations in this field. These are briefly discussed below.

World Peace through World Law

In 1958 Grenville Clark and Louis Sohn wrote their detailed document aimed at the elimination of war, *World Peace through World Law*. Although cast in the form of a revision to the United Nations Charter, its provisions would so radically alter the UN as to cause it to become a world government in many respects. With all the rigorous care of a legal document (the authors were professors of law), it laid out the particulars of a phased, fully-monitored and universal disarmament involving all military weapons, personnel and weapons-producing facilities. It proposed a simultaneous build-up of a world police force with active and reservist divisions adequate to overpower any national, or even multi-national, attempt to act contrary to the will of the world body.

The nations represented in this revised General

Assembly are divided into six categories according to their population, the number of representatives from each country being fixed according to that country's category. Although the smaller nations have fewer representatives, they still have proportionally more representation, thus resolving the question of representation in a unicameral context. The UN Security Council would be replaced by an Executive Council which would be subordinate to the General Assembly and would, therefore, have no veto power. A revised International Court of Justice would have compulsory jurisdiction over all matters that threaten to disrupt the peace, as well as matters relating to the interpretation of the revised charter. A World Development Authority is also proposed, in recognition of the fact that severe economic ills can be as much of a threat to peace as excessive armaments. A revenue system is also envisaged.

Certain elements, however, are missing from the *World Peace through World Law* proposal. Perhaps in an effort to make the proposal more palatable to all sorts of governments, no guarantees of the preservation of human rights were made. Although the revised UN would pledge not to infringe on certain rights of nations or people, it is not empowered to defend anyone's human rights either. This is sure to make some people wary, and justifiably so.

It should also be noted that in this proposal, the revised UN is empowered to deal only with matters relating to peace. While this feature may make the program more acceptable to national leaders, it is certainly clear by now that environmental problems, trade and financial problems, resource shortages, over-population and a host of other problems demand nothing less than the united and fully coordinated response that only a world authority can provide.

Regardless of its shortcomings, the Clark-Sohn proposal has taken its place in history as one of the first serious and detailed attempts to deal with the problem of war through the establishment of a world authority. It is a standard by which other efforts in this area are often judged.

A Constitution for the World

In the years following World War II, several Western scholars of diverse educational fields joined together to produce *A Constitution for the World*. This envisaged a president and a World Council elected by a Federal Convention which was in turn elected by the people of the world. The president would appoint the members of a supreme court. All three branches would have representation in a Chamber of Guardians which would oversee the federal armed forces and set limits on the size of national militias and the manufacturing of all armaments. A 'Declaration of Duties and Rights' includes economic, social, civil and environmental rights as well as the duty of abstaining from violence. (This, interestingly enough, covers the four main areas of international values which, some twenty years later, were recognized by the World Order Models Project.) A Tribune of the People is established to 'defend the natural and civil rights of individuals and groups against violation or neglect by the World Government or any of its component units', including national governments.

The establishment of a world currency, a uniform system of measures, universal compulsory education, the elimination of extremes of poverty and a federal system of taxation are some further elements of the constitution that Bahá'ís would readily endorse. Its writers consciously strove to create a system that would allow for the differences between the capitalist and the communist economic systems, and be acceptable to both of them. The document is shorter than both *World Peace through World Law* and *A Constitution for the Federation of Earth* (discussed below), but various clauses allow for future decisions to be made in the areas that are currently unspecified, making it generally more flexible for changing future conditions.

The *Constitution* is not without faults, however. Perhaps because of the early date at which it was written, when a post-war military demobilization was simply assumed, no provisions for international disarmament are explicitly made. And surprisingly, although the delegates to the Federal Convention are elected in proportion to the population, the representation on the World Council is divided equally among *regions* instead of according to population. The regions with a larger-than-average share of the world's population will surely object to this.

Nevertheless, *A Constitution for the World* takes us much further along the road to world government. Unlike *World Peace through World Law*, its institutions are empowered to regulate world trade, finances and resource distribution, and to create whatever future institutions are needed to deal with other world problems as they arise.

A Constitution for the Federation of Earth

A more recent effort in this direction is being made by

the World Constitution and Parliament Association. Several years of work resulted in the adoption of *A Constitution for the Federation of Earth* at a 'World Constituent Assembly' held in Innsbruck, Austria, in 1977. Participants from twenty-five different countries, from every continent, signed the document. It currently claims a constituency of over four million people. One interesting aspect of the Constitution is that its supporters are actively promoting it for ratification, not only by the various national governments (who tend to be hesitant, of course) but by non-governmental groups of all kinds. Thus it is an effort both to unite mankind and at the same time to educate us about peace and world federation. The steps toward establishing a world government are outlined in the document itself and are being pursued.

This constitution contains all of the basic elements of world government mentioned above. It is broader than either of the two previous proposals. Indeed, some might claim that it goes beyond the bounds of a true federation in some regards. A three chamber parliament draws its representatives from peoples, governments and universities, respectively. Legislation must be passed by any two of the three houses in order to become law. Human rights are clearly delineated and are divided into those which are immediately granted and those which are impractical to grant now, but which the future world order must strive to achieve (called 'directive principles'). The question of bureaucracy is dealt with directly, by providing a 'world ombudsman' or public defender. The principle of unity in diversity is specifically upheld.

Apart from being open to the charge that it goes beyond the bounds of a true federation in some instances, and apart from the world political parties that it envisages, the only other weakness of this constitution, from a Bahá'í point of view, is that its means of disarmament and enforcement seem to be rather poorly defined. Perhaps this is due to the contrast with *World Peace through World Law*, which defines these items in great detail. But one is also tempted to wonder if the authors' aversion to war has prevented them from mandating the forces necessary to create the 'unchallengeable authority' which the world government must have in order to prevent war.

Be that as it may, the *Constitution for the Federation of Earth* represents another major step on the road to world government, and one that is being actively advocated.

Although none of the three constitutions discussed above can be regarded as being perfect, the point is that this goal is being pursued. As more and more thoughtful people consider these documents and recommend additions or changes, the preparatory groundwork for the Lesser Peace is being laid.

Some Additional Thoughts

The abandonment of the war-system of international affairs has many implications, some of which have not been considered in the documents described above. Therefore, a few additional thoughts concerning several of these implications are in order.

The nature of war has changed greatly since the end of World War II. Traditional warfare, in the sense of one government attacking another in order to take over its land and people, occurs less frequently today than it did in the past; and where it does occur, the attacker has seldom been successful. This type of warfare has been largely replaced by the threat of nuclear annihilation on the one hand, and by a myriad of guerrilla wars, coups d'état, acts of terrorism, propaganda campaigns and international intimidation on the other. These more common forms of war today are often supported by outside governments to promote their own geopolitical advantage.

A world government must be so constituted as to be able to prevent not only traditional and nuclear wars, but also these modern forms of war. If it were responsible for protecting basic human rights and guaranteeing justice, much of the legitimate motivation for guerrilla warfare, coups and terrorism would evaporate. Beyond this, a tight control on the production and distribution of light arms and explosives is among the things required to prevent guerrilla warfare. Coups could be avoided if the world government were obligated to re-establish, by force if necessary, any legitimate government that had been illegally toppled. A coordinated world authority devoted to preventing acts of terrorism, and authorized to search any location in any country, is surely one of the most effective means of arresting the terrorists that perpetrate such acts. When it becomes clear that the only effective means of change is through legally constituted channels, when justifiable grievances are treated with justice instead of being ignored, when national governments cease to provide funding and havens for terrorists and guerrillas and when they adopt a universal policy of dealing with, and punishing, such international outlaws, then these forms of modern warfare will cease.

The indirect use of armies to force neighboring

countries into 'cooperation' by intimidation is another aspect of the modern world that must be dealt with by any proposal for world government. It may be that these armies represent a sort of de facto sovereignty which the armed or powerful country holds over its relatively unarmed or weaker neighbors. In order to bring all governments to agreement, it may be necessary to recognize this kind of sovereignty. On the other hand, the unarmed nations may insist on becoming independent. Some sort of semi-autonomous relationship, perhaps scheduled to evolve toward greater independence in stages, supervised by the world government and guided by world law, may prove to be a solution to this difficult problem.

It would be very difficult to outlaw political propaganda, in which one state attempts to influence the politics of another, if freedom of the press is to be guaranteed. However, although a free press may not necessarily be unbiased, at least its biases lean in several directions, between which the truth can usually be found. In countries where the means to effect change is made legally available to its citizens, such propaganda has a less significant effect. A world government would undoubtedly seek to increase the number of these countries as part of its program of extending human rights. Furthermore, worldwide increases in the literacy rate, and in the level of education in general, will make successful propaganda programs difficult, if not impossible, to achieve.

As to the question of human rights, it would certainly be easier to simply sidestep the issue, as some have tried to do, by leaving it on the national level. But this cannot be done for several reasons. The questions of guaranteeing existing freedoms and of providing a common basis of international values have already been mentioned. Human rights guarantees are also required in order to prevent institutionalized injustices which are often the initial cause of guerrilla warfare, coups d'état and terrorism.

The coup d'état is a particularly interesting case. There are two reasons why any proposed world government must outlaw this form of 'warfare'. First of all, if its continued existence were allowed, then the most powerful nations might seek to use it for their own geopolitical gain. It could very easily replace guerrilla warfare in the same way that guerrilla warfare has largely replaced traditional warfare. This would undermine the legitimacy of the world legislature. Secondly, since the central purpose of the world government is to provide peace and security for the whole world, how can it ignore the coup? The coup is a greater threat to the security of Third World nations than either nuclear or traditional warfare. Third World leaders will rightly reject as irrelevant any proposed world government that is not empowered to prevent the coup d'état. This role of world government is essential if it is to solve *all* of the problems that armed conflict formerly solved.

The elimination of this threat is not difficult. The world government could simply act as a guarantor to the national governments, providing a superior external force that would quickly remove any illegitimate government that comes to power in a coup. But a major problem arises: if basic human rights are not guaranteed, then the world government could become the guarantor for some very oppressive national governments. If coup is the only *real* means of change in some countries, to eliminate it without replacing it with a legitimate means of change would be to invite oppression.

In short, to guarantee peace, particularly in the Third World, we must guarantee human rights.

The question of human rights, however, is a very delicate one. While it is essential that they be explicitly listed and safeguarded, nations disagree on which rights are important. Communist nations provide certain economic and social rights while ignoring civil and political ones. Capitalist nations think of the civil/ political rights as being essential and not the others. Both groups feel that the inclusion of the additional sets of rights would alter their societies too greatly, and hence they resist all change in this area. Third World leaders would often like to provide more of both types of rights to their people, but find themselves unable to provide either, due to economic and security constraints.

One possible response to this dilemma is to establish a standard, comprehensive set of rights that would come into force worldwide over a long period, say fifty years, and according to a definite timetable for each nation. This timetable would be drawn up separately for each nation, taking into account the individual circumstances of that nation. Thus, the effect of the changes would not cause any sudden disruptions, and the leaders who initially agree to the program need not feel that their own positions are threatened. The timetable would serve to assure people that the changes are indeed coming and are being handled in a planned, orderly fashion. The world government would ensure that the timetable was enforced.

Bahá'ís recognize the principle of the 'immutable law of change', that everything is either growing, improving, gathering, or dispersing and dying.[6] As applied to governments, this means that they must have sufficient flexibility to respond to change. Many of the problems of civil and political rights arise because of governmental unwillingness to respond to changing circumstances. An important stage in each nation's human rights program is reached when the national government becomes responsive to the legitimate demands for changes in policy by the majority of its people. (This does not necessarily mean that it has to be a democracy, particularly in countries where the system of democracy is culturally foreign.) Once a country has provided the legitimate channels for change the world government could offer to be the guarantor of such a government against coups or other illegitimate internal threats. This offer would encourage national governments, particularly in the Third World, to accept and implement more civil and political rights.

The question of human rights has not been ignored by the world at large. Since the worldwide acceptance of the Universal Declaration of Human Rights in 1948, the number of conferences that have studied the many aspects of human rights, the number of human rights declarations and conventions that have been promoted and accepted, the number of scholars, lawyers, diplomats and writers that have devoted their time to this field, and the general consciousness of mankind in this area have all grown dramatically. Although an enforceable worldwide convention has not yet emerged, a tremendous amount of the groundwork for this important aspect of world government has already been laid.[7]

Another question that is worthy of further study is

that of the holding of elections for the members of the world parliament from countries that have no historical experience in holding genuine elections. If there is to be a chamber of the parliament that represents 'the people', then such elections seem essential. It will probably be necessary for a world government not only to set the standard guidelines for the elections, but to supervise them as well. How the first election will take place will require careful consideration and consultation. Nations which are new to this kind of electoral process might well learn from it and eventually apply it locally.

It is often imagined that the establishment of world government implies that all people would be free to move and settle wherever they please. A little reflection on this matter, however, makes it clear that this is not necessarily so. As long as some nations remain extremely wealthy while others are poor, the opening of all national borders could cause millions of people to flood into the wealthy countries. Social chaos in both types of nations would be the likely result. The goal of eliminating all border restrictions is a worthy one, but not necessarily one that can be implemented immediately. However, as the world's wealth becomes more evenly distributed among the nations in a world system, due in part to the application of the economic aspects of human rights and the elimination of the costs of war, the economic pressure to relocate should be reduced and border regulations could be diminished and eventually eliminated.

The establishment of world government also implies some major occupational changes, which are bound to be one source of resistance to the idea of world government. Primarily, it will be necessary to transfer several million military personnel into the civilian economy, and to re-train many of them for new jobs. It will mean that the armaments industry will come to a complete halt, which, given its multi-billion dollar size, will have some major economic consequences. Diplomats and other members of the foreign service will also find their roles changed greatly.[8] These and other occupational changes will cause some short term disruptions, some of which could be spread out over a longer period in order to minimize their impact. However, the long term advantages of spending large sums on uplifting mankind instead of perfecting armies and weapons are incalculable.

When the world congress is convened to establish a world government, it is to be hoped that the participants would include not only political leaders and statesmen, but also the leaders of thought and vision who recognize some of the new realities of the age in which we live. It will be essential to have some true 'world citizens' there, whose desire for a universal and lasting peace overrides any ideological leanings that they might have. If the participants dedicate themselves to the well-being of the whole earth above and beyond any local allegiances or ideologies, then they will have set an excellent example for the members of the world government to follow. Such an atmosphere of world consciousness is essential for the successful completion of their sacred task.

Chapter IV

GETTING THERE

After outlining the various advantages of world government, refuting the supposed disadvantages based on fear or skepticism, and after illustrating some of the proposed models, one often gets a response such as, 'This is all very fine in theory; but in the *real world*, how do we get there from here?' No discussion about world government can be complete without addressing this vitally important question.

Broadly speaking, Bahá'ís recognize that there are two possible futures immediately ahead. One is that mankind will become sufficiently aware of its extremely dangerous predicament, will overcome a sufficient amount of its materialism, its prejudices and its fears, and will find sufficient willpower, to establish a true world government before the occurrence of some sort of major economic, ecological or nuclear-derived collapse of the whole world system. The other future is that we do not act in time and that we must therefore rely upon the spiritually chastening effects of such a global catastrophe to empower us to throw off our old ways and establish a world government.

On the other hand, there are two commonly held views of the world's future that Bahá'ís specifically do not accept. The first is that the world will somehow be able forever to continue muddling its way through world problems using nation-oriented solutions. This view is clearly denied in some of the Bahá'í quotations already cited. At the other end of the spectrum, the view that all of mankind will be destroyed in a holocaust of some sort is implicitly rejected by the numerous prophecies concerning the Most Great Peace, the kingdom of God on earth, and so on, none of which could be fulfilled without people. If it can be shown, for example, that a full-scale nuclear war would certainly destroy all of mankind, then we as Bahá'ís know that such a war will not take place. This does not preclude the possibility of a less-than-full-scale war that nevertheless could destroy a large portion of humanity.

Peace Education

Ideally, the efforts which we put forth toward establishing world peace should be such that they produce beneficial results regardless of whether the world chooses the high road of initiative or the low road of suffering as its path to world peace. Efforts in the realm of educating people for world peace meet this criterion.

'Abdu'l-Bahá makes it clear that peace and unity among people must first occur in their minds, which is essentially a process of education, '. . . for until the minds of men become united, no important matter can be accomplished. At present universal peace is a matter of great importance, but unity of conscience is essential, so that the foundation of this matter may become secure, its establishment firm and its edifice strong.'[1]

History also points to the importance of first obtaining a broad basis of support on this issue:

Woodrow Wilson's failure [to convince the USA to join the League of Nations] illustrates this second point. His design for the League of Nations began with the presumption of elite support. He depended upon congres-

sional elites to share his vision. But without having first
created a national forum for raising the consciousness of
the voters, Wilson saw his statesmanship torpedoed in a
Congress that, sensing little grass-roots support, could
claim the people were 'not ready'. Today's world-order
movement must avoid this mistake.[2]

Education for peace has many facets. It is necessary to
demonstrate to people the seriousness of the world's
situation, and to show that solutions are required that
are based on world cooperation and world government
instead of on nationalistic feelings. It is necessary to
demonstrate that world government is not a hopeless
dream but a practical possibility. But it is also necessary
to teach people about peace in the broader sense of
recognizing the oneness of mankind, striving to eliminate the hatreds, prejudices and fears of each other,
accepting the validity of alien cultures, being willing
to share the world's resources in a more equitable
manner, respecting people of different religions or
philosophies, and abandoning old concepts of action
according to dictatorial power, while accepting the
more modern concept of problem-solving by cooperation and consultation.

The task is certainly an immense one. But fortunately Bahá'ís are not alone. In addition to the numerous
groups working for world peace and disarmament,
there are many organizations that specifically recognize
the importance of establishing a world government in
the near future. The World Federalists Association is
probably the best known. Planetary Citizens is perhaps
the largest single group, with a membership of 200,000.
The World Citizens Assembly, The Campaign for
World Government, and the World Constitution and
Parliament Association are some of the others in the

USA.[3] One also finds the World Citizens Party of West Germany, the World Union of India, the World Citizens Center of Canada and similar organizations in many countries. Some organizations, such as the Parliamentarians for World Order, and the International Registry of World Citizens, are truly international in scope.

In addition to these organizations, there are a great many other groups that are concerned with peace or disarmament but do not yet recognize the linkage between these causes and world government. Large and diverse segments of the populations of the USA and Western Europe are actively concerned about disarmament, as is evident from the participation in the anti-nuclear protests on both continents in recent years. An even greater number of concerned people are working for progressive organizations which are trying to deal with poverty, pollution, crime, education, medical care, housing, drug abuse, divorce, child abuse, etc., and are increasingly frustrated by their inability to achieve their goals because of the drain on resources caused by the cost of 'defense'.[4] These and others are coming closer to the recognition that the problem of unity must be solved first, and that the other problems of mankind are often but symptoms of this basic disease.

Another very important aspect of peace education is the education of children, for there is no doubt that age-old fears and prejudices could be entirely overturned in a single generation if children were properly educated. This is emphasized in *The Promise of World Peace*, which adds that 'consideration should also be given to teaching the concept of world citizenship as part of the standard education of every child.'[5] Although the immediate effects of this type of effort seem small, the long range effects would be very far-reaching, especially if initiated in an age such as ours which is so ripe for change. The children that are in school today will be the young adults at the opening of the twenty-first century. They will have a great influence on the character of the newly emergent new world order.

Mankind still has the choice of which path to take to world peace. A peaceful resolution to the dilemma is still within our collective capability. *The Promise of World Peace* states:

The Great Peace . . . is now at long last within the reach of the nations . . .
  Whether peace is to be reached only after unimaginable horrors precipitated by humanity's stubborn clinging to old patterns of behaviour, or is to be embraced now by an act of consultative will, is the choice before all who inhabit the earth.[6]

  Beyond peace education and widening the base of support for world government, several strategies have already been devised by others for converting that support into political action which would promote the gradual transfer of the international aspects of national sovereignty to a supranational organization.[7]

The Path of Suffering

Although the path of initiative and cooperation is still possible, it has appeared to many observers, Bahá'í and non-Bahá'í alike, that mankind is more likely to choose the path of suffering in order to reach world peace. Thus, one often finds references in the Bahá'í Writings to some sort of a great calamity that is likely to befall mankind unless it shakes off its heedlessness and more fully accepts the teachings of God for our age. I would like to explore this area not only because it is our possible, perhaps even probable, future, but because it is an area which is seldom explored, particularly by non-Bahá'í writers, who tend to think only in terms of mankind's total avoidance of nuclear war or his total destruction by it.

It should be noted, when speaking of this calamity, that the real calamity has already occurred, and continues to occur, as both the people of the world and its leaders hear of God's Messenger and choose to reject Him. This is the great spiritual calamity which has already largely taken place. But it is also true that the physical world is a reflection of the spiritual world in a great number of ways. Hence the spiritual calamity of the rejection of God's message is likely to lead to an equivalent calamity in the physical realm. Some of the passages in the Bahá'í Writings may refer to the spiritual calamity; others may refer to the turbulence of the entire period from the dawn of the Bahá'í Revelation to the coming of the Most Great Peace. But some, particularly those of the Guardian, seem to refer to a specific forthcoming event.

After describing the need for a federated world government in 'The Goal of a New World Order', the Guardian commented on the probable means of its establishment:

That so fundamental a revolution, involving such far-reaching changes in the structure of society, can be achieved through the ordinary processes of diplomacy and education seems highly improbable. We have but to turn our gaze to humanity's blood-stained history to realize that nothing short of intense mental as well as physical agony has been able to precipitate those epoch-making changes that constitute the greatest landmarks in the history of human civilization.

Great and far-reaching as have been those changes in the past, they cannot appear, when viewed in their proper perspective, except as subsidiary adjustments preluding that transformation of unparalleled majesty and scope which humanity is in this age bound to undergo. That the forces of a world catastrophe can alone precipitate such a new phase of human thought is, alas, becoming increasingly apparent. That nothing short of the fire of a severe ordeal, unparalleled in its intensity, can fuse and weld the discordant entities that constitute the elements of present-day civilization, into the integral components of the world commonwealth of the future, is a truth which future events will increasingly demonstrate.

The prophetic voice of Bahá'u'lláh warning, in the concluding passages of the Hidden Words, 'the peoples of the world' that 'an unforeseen calamity is following them and that grievous retribution awaiteth them' throws indeed a lurid light upon the immediate fortunes of sorrowing humanity. Nothing but a fiery ordeal, out of which humanity will emerge, chastened and prepared, can succeed in implanting that sense of responsibility which the leaders of a new-born age must arise to shoulder.[8]

Although this passage was written before World War II, and although that war motivated mankind to establish the United Nations, the death of fifty-five million people proved to be insufficient to cause mankind to abandon the nation-state system in favor of a true world government. Thus the Guardian characterized World War II as simply a 'foretaste' of things to come. In 1954 he wrote:

Indeed a foretaste of the devastation which this consuming fire will wreak upon the world, and with which it will lay waste the cities of the nations participating in this tragic world-engulfing contest, has been afforded by the last World War, marking the second stage in the global havoc which humanity, forgetful of its God and heedless of the clear warnings uttered by His appointed Messenger for this day, must, alas, inevitably experience.[9]

In the case of the United States in particular, he linked the inevitable tribulations with the establishment of world government:

Tribulations, on a scale unprecedented in its [US] history, and calculated to purge its institutions, to purify the hearts of its people, to fuse its constituent elements, and to weld it into one entity with its sister nations in both hemispheres, are inevitable.[10]

Drawing upon 'Abdu'l-Bahá's observation after the close of World War I that the League of Nations would be incapable of keeping the peace inasmuch as 'the fire of unquenched hatreds still smoulders in their hearts',[11] might we not reach a conclusion similar to His, that 'another war, fiercer than the last, will assuredly break out'?[12]

One of the unfortunate lessons of history is that mankind tends to resist necessary change, often waiting until the existing order collapses before changes of any significance are accepted. Today this policy is expressed, in positive terms, as 'incrementalism'. It says that 'as long as there is nothing major that is clearly collapsing, all adjustments to the system should be minor in order to allow us to evaluate whether the adjustments are positive or negative and to make future moves accordingly'. While this policy seems reasonable on the surface, it specifically precludes the possibility of peaceful structural change, which by its nature is major. While policy-makers are busily attending to the surface conditions, the structure below is rotting away. In the case of the re-structuring of international relations, it is clear that all of the significant progress in this century has come only *after* the two most destructive wars the world has ever known. Heedless of this fact, the world today seems to be following the same policy and to be heading toward further structural change by the same sorry method.

'The whole earth', Bahá'u'lláh said, 'is now in a state of pregnancy.'[13] Indeed, the analogy is an apt one. Birth, by its very nature, is non-incremental. The world has been experiencing periodic and ever increasing pains. Although its change in condition may have been relatively gradual in the past, sooner or later a very non-gradual event, painful but essential, seems destined to occur, marking the birth of a new world order.

Concerning the willingness of nations to accept change, one additional aspect should be noted. While each of the World Wars has awakened mankind to the need for a change in the system of international affairs, neither one motivated the ruling powers sufficiently to cause them to give up part of their sovereignty in favor of a world government. And the reason for this seems clear enough: at the end of a war, the defeated nations are willing to accept any new system, even if it includes the loss of their sovereignty – indeed, they have no choice. Sharing sovereignty in a world government is a benign solution, as far as they are concerned. But the 'victorious' nations, revelling in their victory, are hardly in a mood to give up any of their sovereignty to a world government. Quite the opposite: they are ready to use their newly-proven sovereignty to dictate the terms under which the post-war world will operate. This is illustrated by the attitude of the leading powers during the formation of the United Nations. In 1946, the Soviet representative to the UN, Andrei Gromyko, said:

When the Charter of the United Nations was prepared by the conference at San Francisco, the question of sovereignty was one of the most important questions considered. This principle of sovereignty is one of the cornerstones on which the United Nations structure is built; if this were touched the whole existence and future of the United Nations would be threatened.[14]

A similar view was held by the American side, as was made evident in an episode that occurred at the same conference. Several people realized from the beginning the significance of the Security Council and the veto power of its permanent members: that despite the high-sounding aims and principles of the UN, the leading world powers would reserve final authority for themselves. The chief delegate from the Philippines was one such person. He 'fought against the veto until he was pointedly told by the US that there would be no UN unless the veto was included.'[15]

It would seem, therefore, that not only are the nations unwilling to move toward greater unity except after a major war, but that even after such a war the establishment of world government is impossible as long as there are victorious nations. If this pattern continues, then the only route to world government is not simply through war, but through a war which has no winners. By a seemingly curious coincidence, mankind appears to be headed toward precisely such a war. Such destruction as could only have occurred through supernatural forces when it was prophesied in the past became possible with the advent of nuclear weapons in 1945, and has ever since become more and more probable, to such an extent that many modern observers wonder if it is not inevitable.

However, neither the exact nature of this calamity nor its timing are clearly indicated in the Bahá'í

Writings. Although war, particularly nuclear war, seems to fit the description in several ways, other forms of calamity are not ruled out: environmental collapse, chemical or biological warfare, falling asteroids from outer space, or some other calamity that is totally unforeseen. In most regards, it is a moot point. An unparalleled calamity is an unparalleled calamity, regardless of its nature. A description without a name is sufficient.

As to its magnitude, in addition to the passages of the Guardian already cited, Bahá'u'lláh wrote that, 'The hour is approaching when the most great convulsion will have appeared.'[16] The Guardian speaks of 'a universal commotion, of a scope and intensity unparalleled in the annals of mankind.'[17] Indeed, it seems possible that the following prophecies of Jesus may refer to the same convulsion:

For then there will be great tribulation, such as has not been from the beginning of the world until now, no, and never will be. And if those days had not been shortened, no human being would be saved; but for the sake of the elect those days will be shortened . . . As were the days of Noah, so will be the coming of the Son of man. For as in those days before the flood they were eating and drinking, marrying and giving in marriage, until the day when Noah entered the ark, and they did not know until the flood came and swept them all away, so will be the coming of the Son of man.[18]

The Guardian himself speaks of us as building 'that Ark of human salvation, ordained as the ultimate haven of a society destined, for the most part, to be submerged by the tidal wave of the abuses and evils which its own perversity has engendered.'[19]

The purpose of the calamity of Noah's age was the same as its purpose is today: to cause us to abandon materialism and advance spiritually. If man rejects every other means of spiritual advancement, then God seems to be willing to allow mankind to carry this rejection to its natural conclusion – a collapse of his material civilization. It is at once a 'retribution' for man's failure to accept God's Messenger, a 'cleansing process' intended to exorcise his perversity, and a constructive step necessary to 'weld [humanity's] component parts into one organic, indivisible world-embracing community'.[20]

The image of fire is frequently used in the description of the calamity: 'If carried to excess, civilization will prove as prolific a source of evil as it had been of goodness when kept within the restraints of moderation . . . The day is approaching when its flame will devour the cities. . . '[21] The 'burning of cities' is listed by the Guardian in his last Riḍván message as one of sixteen things that would 'either herald or accompany the retributive calamity'.[22] Passages such as, 'Soon shall the blasts of His chastisement beat upon you, and the dust of hell enshroud you',[23] have an ominous ring to those who are familiar with the effects of nuclear weapons. The Guardian seems specifically to anticipate the possibility of a nuclear war between the Soviet Union and the United States in his 1954 letter entitled 'American Bahá'ís in the Time of World Peril'.[24] Again, when looking at the probable future of the 'advanced peoples' versus that of the villagers of the world, one is tempted to wonder how literal will be the fulfillment of Jesus's statement 'Blessed are the meek, for they shall inherit the earth'.[25]

Nor are the Bahá'ís alone in recognizing the very dangerous predicament of the present situation: 'I am terrified by having to admit', says Carl-Friedrich von

Weizsacker, 'that it is increasingly probable that this step [of creating a world government] will be taken only as the result of an atomic world war, for the reasons already given.'[26] (He had earlier shown that all three scenarios of an arms race, an arms halt, and disarmament without world government, are likely to lead eventually to a nuclear war.) Richard Falk, in the preface to *This Endangered Planet*, states, 'Unless the political leadership in the United States, the Soviet Union, China, Japan, India, and "Europe" come to understand and act upon these conditions of planetary peril within this century, there is little hope that our children will avoid the apocalypse.'[27] He later adds that, 'There is little evidence that any change in the structure of world order is likely to come about in the years ahead, unless it is provoked by a catastrophe of awesome proportion.'[28] Hermann Kahn wrote in 1960 that '. . . it is most doubtful in the absence of a crisis or war that a world government can be set up in the next decade.'[29] This statement is certainly just as true today.

How Do We Respond?

The acknowledgment of such a probable future is devastating, even unthinkable, to most people today – particularly those whose philosophy of materialism teaches them to regard their possessions, pastimes and pleasures as the only things of real significance. Disbelief that such a thing could happen is the most frequent response of those who regard their life in this world as the sum total of their existence. Those who do manage to acknowledge the likelihood of this outcome, particularly among the younger generation, are paralyzed by the thought either of having no future, or of having one that is so radically different from the present that no normal present-day actions are meaningful.

Bahá'ís, of course, must avoid both of these pitfalls. We can not blithely dismiss the clear warnings all around us, nor can we be paralyzed by the thoughts of the great changes and tests that appear to be coming, nor can we allow the darkness of the near future to dim our vision of that glorious future which is destined to emerge at the end of these years of upheaval.

Our ability to face such a future arises directly from the Bahá'í world-view, which is so completely different from that of those around us. Recognizing, as we do, that our life in this world is but a small portion of our total existence, the thought of its being radically altered or shortened does not have the significance that it does to others. In becoming Bahá'ís, we have dedicated our lives to God's Cause, and have, in a sense, already lost our lives. (Certainly the materialist would agree!) We seek to become tools in God's hands, and as such, leave it to His wisdom as to how long He will use us in this world and just when and how He will move us to the next.

Bahá'u'lláh asks that each of His servants should be raised up 'to such heights that he will regard the world even as a shadow that vanisheth swifter than the twinkling of an eye'.[30] Such detachment from the material world, such a spiritual outlook, will prove to be essential if we are to cope with the radical changes in the physical world that seem likely to occur. Tremenddous tests, both mental and physical, will have to be endured. But unlike most people around us, we know that they have a purpose, and that beyond them is the greatest period of peace and spiritual growth that the world has ever witnessed. And in this knowledge lies our optimism and our strength.

Indeed, we must see all things with spiritual eyes in order to be able to provide hope to mankind when all others have lost hope. We must be able to provide a vision of a positive future world when all manmade visions are forgotten. And we must be able to provide faith to a faithless generation.

The period between 1844 and the coming of the Lesser Peace is characterized by the Guardian as 'a tempest, unprecedented in its violence'. He summarizes our relationship to this tempest in the following passage, every phrase of which is worthy of our meditation, especially in these turbulent years:

Dear friends! The powerful operations of this titanic upheaval are comprehensible to none except such as have recognized the claims of both Bahá'u'lláh and the Báb. Their followers know full well whence it comes, and what it will ultimately lead to. Though ignorant of how far it will reach, they clearly recognize its genesis, are aware of its direction, acknowledge its necessity, observe confidently its mysterious processes, ardently pray for the mitigation of its severity, intelligently labor to assuage its fury, and anticipate, with undimmed vision, the consummation of the fears and the hopes it must necessarily engender.[31]

But what, then, should we do for the present? What course of action is reasonable in a world whose future is likely to be totally different from its present? As we draw nearer to the end of the century, more and more decisions about the future are likely to be affected by these important considerations.

First of all, let it be said that we can never allow our positive efforts, in any field, to slacken due to a fear that they may not bear fruit. Whether in our education, our careers, our family life or our service to the Cause, we must trust in God that sooner or later, all good actions will yield their benefit.

Among such good actions, the spreading of the Bahá'í teachings about the oneness of mankind in general, and about the feasibility of world government in particular, is surely one of the ones required. Such peace education could lead to the establishment of a world government before some sort of a calamity occurs. But even if it does not, the ability to establish a true world government after the next calamity will depend directly upon the number of people who are ready and willing to abandon the nation-state system at that time. Indeed many people, including the Guardian, had hoped that World War II would be enough to bring about a true world government.[32] But unfortunately, at the end of the war there were still too few leaders and people who both recognized that the problem of war grows directly out of the nation-state system and were willing to act on that recognition. If an unrepentant humanity still clings to its old ways after the next calamity, as it did in 1945, then still further chaos, confusion and suffering will continue to afflict mankind. If a war sets us back technologically, but fails to cause us to progress spiritually in terms of recognizing our unity, then we can be certain that the destroyed technology will eventually be re-invented, and mankind will return to the same dilemma in which it finds itself today. 'It is not the *quantity* of the remnant that is significant', said one observer, reflecting on this theme, 'but its *quality*.' Thus we can see the great importance of promoting the oneness of mankind and the feasibility of world government during the present period.

It is also essential that the Bahá'í teachings be spread as widely as possible prior to the calamity, since they contain within them the very seeds of the future world. The widespread character of the Faith will help to assure that it will continually be able to offer mankind the spiritual food for which it is starving. As the Guardian explained to one of the National Assemblies in Africa:

It is our duty to redeem as many of our fellow-men as we possibly can, whose hearts are enlightened, before some great catastrophe overtakes them, in which they will either be hopelessly swallowed up or come out purified and strengthened, and ready to serve. The more believers there are to stand forth as beacons in the darkness whenever that time does come, the better; hence the supreme importance of the teaching work at this time.[33]

It is especially important to spread the teachings, including those on peace and world government, in the developing countries and among the world's villagers, who are likely to be less directly affected by a calamity due to their distance from the civilization which has overstepped 'the bounds of moderation'. The importance of these regions may grow immeasurably if these people are indeed the 'meek' who 'shall inherit the earth'.

This does not mean that the Bahá'í work in other parts of the world can slacken. Shoghi Effendi assures us, for instance, that in spite of the calamity, America 'will continue to evolve, undivided and undefeatable, until the sum total of its contributions to the birth, the rise and the fruition of that world civilization . . . will have been made, and its last task discharged'.[34] Obviously, Bahá'ís will be needed everywhere to offer God-given solutions to the whole of the human race when all the man-made ones have failed.

In all countries, whether developed or developing, it is essential that both local and national communities be so firmly-grounded that they will continue to function, to teach, to set goals and to grow even if they are cut off from contact with other communities or administrative centers.

The Universal House of Justice is clearly concerned with promoting the transition to world government. The problem is being attacked on several fronts simultaneously, and this is reflected in the goals of recent teaching plans. In response to a question asking what the believers could do in order to help ensure the establishment of a world government, the Universal House of Justice in January 1983 wrote:

Concerning the transition from the present system of national sovereignty to a system of world government, the House of Justice fully agrees with your view that the Bahá'ís must now do all in their power to promote this transition. This requires several related activities . . . One is the establishment as rapidly as possible of firmly grounded efficiently functioning Local Spiritual Assemblies in every part of the world, so that seekers everywhere will have a point of reference to which they can turn for guidance and for the Teachings of the Faith. A second is the deepening of the believers, of all ages, in their understanding of and obedience to the Teachings. A third is the proclamation of the Faith to all strata of society, and in particular to those in authority and to leaders of thought so that those who hold the direction of peoples in their hands will learn accurately about the nature and tenets of the Faith and will grow to respect it and implement its principles. A fourth is the promotion of Bahá'í scholarship, so that an increasing number of believers will be able to analyse the problems of mankind in every field and to show how the Teachings solve them. A fifth is the development of relations between the Bahá'í

International Community and the United Nations both directly with the highest UN institutions and at a grass-roots level in areas of rural development, education, etc. [35]

In addition to wondering what we can do to best serve mankind at this critical juncture in history, questions inevitably arise as to what, if any, physical preparations can be made for such an uncertain future. This obviously depends on where in the world one is living, as well as the exact nature of the calamity. Clearly, devoting all of one's time and resources to building one's own personal bomb-shelter is not within the realm of reasonable action. Not only does it prevent us from doing the more important work of healing the sickness that has caused the problem, but it offers us no guarantee of survival in the first place. Furthermore, it joins us to those who believe that this earthly life is the only thing that is worthy of importance. This is not to say that there is anything wrong with taking some basic precautions, which could prove to be helpful in a variety of circumstances, but simply that the extent of these efforts should not prevent us from doing what is ultimately the most important work of all.

Not long after the beginning of the nuclear arms race, the Guardian asked the American Bahá'ís for a 'veritable exodus from the large cities where a considerable number of believers have, over a period of years, congregated', referring to them as cities 'over which unsuspected dangers are hanging'. [36] Although it is clear that the whole world will be affected by such a calamity, it also seems clear that some areas will be affected more directly than others. A letter written on behalf of the Guardian in the same year further illuminates this theme:

He does not feel that the Bahá'ís should waste time

dwelling on the dark side of things. Any intelligent person can understand from the experiences of the last world war, and keeping abreast of what modern science has developed in the way of weapons for any future war, that big cities all over the world are going to be in tremendous danger. This is what the Guardian has said to the pilgrims.

Entirely aside from this, he has urged the [American] Bahá'ís, for the sake of serving the Faith, to go out from these centers of intense materialism, where life nowadays is so hurried and grinding and, dispersing to towns and villages, carry the Message far and wide throughout the cities of the American Union. He strongly believes that the field outside the big cities is more fertile, that the Bahá'ís in the end will be happier for having made this move, and that, in case of an outbreak of war, it stands to reason they will be safer, just the way any other person living in the country, or away from the big industrial areas, is safer.

It is remarks such as these that the pilgrims have carried back in their notes. He sees no cause for alarm, but he certainly believes that the Bahá'ís should weigh these thoughts, and take action for the sake of spreading the Faith of Bahá'u'lláh, and for their own ultimate happiness as well. Indeed the two things go together.[37]

Thus the appropriate Bahá'í response must be one that combines a very mature spiritual outlook with wise courses of action based on our knowledge of both the present needs and the various possible future situations. It recognizes not only the vital importance of spreading the healing teachings of the Faith as far and wide as possible, but also the great variety of ways and places in which other forms of service to the Cause are required. While not ignoring the fact that humanity's immediate future is 'dark, distressingly dark', it focuses on a somewhat more distant future which is 'gloriously radiant – so radiant that no eye can visualize it'.[38]

Chapter V

CONCLUSIONS

The problem of war, like many other problems, has been with us for centuries. But unlike most of those other problems, the combined efforts of the people of the twentieth century seem unable to resolve it. Our modern technology has put within our reach worldwide solutions to the problems of poverty, ignorance and illness, yet it has only aggravated the problem of war. So many of our resources are devoted to preparation for war that other problems, which could be easily solved, are left unattended. War remains like a deep and festering wound in the body of mankind which man has, so far, been unwilling to treat. It will continue to cause mankind both chronic and acute pain until its true cause – attachment to the nation-state system – is completely rooted out.

'Abdu'l-Bahá said:

Every century holds the solution of one predominating problem. Although there may be many problems, yet one of the innumerable problems will loom large and become the most important of all . . . In this luminous century the greatest bestowal of the world of humanity is Universal Peace, which must be founded, so that the realm of creation may obtain composure, the East and the West, which include in their arms the five continents of the globe, may embrace each other, mankind may rest beneath the tent of oneness of the world of humanity, and the flag of universal peace may wave over all the regions.[1]

Future generations will not see the twentieth century in terms of East versus West, nor in terms of communist versus capitalist versus fascist. Rather, they will look back on this century and see it in terms of the struggle between the forces of world disunity and those of world unity, between the forces of death and those of life, between attachment to our past and the destiny that is our future. They will see the international organizations that followed each of the World Wars as being successive steps in the birth of a new world order, and the first glimmerings of world civilization. The significance of our times will not be lost on them, for they will surely look back on it as one of the greatest and most dramatic periods in the history of mankind. It is our privilege to live in such an age, our challenge to face its unique tests, and our special bounty, as Bahá'ís, to understand its true significance.

For the present, one of the most urgent tasks at hand is to spread the idea of the necessity and the feasibility of world government. Since true and lasting peace is inseparably linked to world law, the notion of peace without world government can never be anything more than a mirage. A world authority, with adequate power to make and enforce laws between the nations, is an indispensable requirement for world peace.

Part of the process of learning about peace is simply recognizing that the world around us has already become united in many functional respects. The tele-mass inventions have removed the distances between us and have created a new reality with which limited national institutions are incapable of dealing. In creating these inventions, we have become the giants of the earth. We have had the courage, the strength and the vision to develop the giant systems of transportation and communication that have so radically altered our world. We cannot, we must not, fail to have the courage, the strength and the vision to build the giant organizational structure that alone can adequately regulate the affairs of the new world which we have created.

Skepticism or fear are the commonly found emotional responses to the concept of world government. Although they are backed up by a variety of arguments, none of these is truly valid. In spreading the idea of world government, it will be necessary for us to fight fear with courage, and to push back skepticism with faith, confidence and vision. For the typical and easy responses of fear and skepticism are yet another facet of that spiritual disease which has afflicted much of mankind.

The task is formidable, but we are not alone in recognizing the problem and its proper solution. There are many organizations that promote the establishment of a world federal government. Several detailed proposals, in the form of 'world constitutions' have already been written. Spreading the idea of world government as a realistic solution to the problem of war is an essential prerequisite to its establishment, regardless of whether or not man responds quickly enough to avert the world's next major calamity.

Certainly, there are scenarios by which a sufficient number of people would respond to the idea in time, motivating national governments to establish friendlier relationships and, eventually, a world government. Let us pray that our efforts to educate people might lead to such a scenario. But in terms of probability, this seems to be the less likely route. The following lines, written a few years prior to the last World War, sound so appropriate for our present situation that one is tempted to wonder whether we might not be at a similar point on the war–peace cycle as when the Guardian wrote them:

Every system, short of the unification of the human race, has been tried, repeatedly tried, and been found wanting. Wars again and again have been fought, and conferences without number have met and deliberated. Treaties, pacts and covenants have been painstakingly negotiated, concluded and revised. Systems of government have been patiently tested, have been continually recast and superseded. Economic plans of reconstruction have been carefully devised, and meticulously executed. And yet crisis has succeeded crisis, and the rapidity with which a perilously unstable world is declining has been correspondingly accelerated. A yawning gulf threatens to involve [mankind] in one common disaster. . .[2]

And yet we hold out the hope that after such a disaster mankind will not fail to learn from its mistakes, and that it will take every necessary step required to abolish war by establishing a federal government for our planet.

Ultimately, the lesson that mankind must learn in this age, is that the price of peace is not billions of dollars for ever more destructive weapons; nor is it a trillion dollars for defenses in space. The price of peace is not acceptance of a policy of 'Mutual Assured Destruction'; nor is it acceptance of a multitude of 'little' wars scattered about various corners of the globe. What mankind desperately needs to learn is that the price of peace is national sovereignty, and not all of its national sovereignty at that. War will continue, at one level or another, until the nations relinquish their lawlessness and learn to become law-abiding citizens in the country of Earth. And the sooner mankind learns how to do this, the better for us all.

BIBLIOGRAPHY

'Abdu'l-Bahá in Canada. Ontario: National Spiritual Assembly of the Bahá'ís of Canada, 1962.

'Abdu'l-Bahá. *Paris Talks*. London: Bahá'í Publishing Trust, 1972.

—— *The Promulgation of Universal Peace*. Wilmette, Illinois: Bahá'í Publishing Trust, 1982.

—— *The Secret of Divine Civilization*. Wilmette, Illinois: Bahá'í Publishing Trust, 1970.

—— *Selections from the Writings of 'Abdu'l-Bahá*. Translated by a Committee at the Bahá'í World Centre and by Marzieh Gail. Haifa: Bahá'í World Centre, 1978.

—— *Some Answered Questions*. Collected and translated from the Persian by Laura Clifford Barney. Wilmette, Illinois: Bahá'í Publishing Trust, 1981.

Akey, Denise S., ed. *Encyclopedia of Associations 1985*. Detroit, Michigan: Gale Research Co., 1984.

Anderson, Sir Robert. *The Coming Prince*. Grand Rapids, Michigan: Kregal Publications, 1983.

Bahá'í Prayers. A Selection of Prayers Revealed by Bahá'u'lláh, The Báb and 'Abdu'l-Bahá. Wilmette, Illinois: Bahá'í Publishing Trust, 1982.

Bahá'u'lláh. *Gleanings from the Writings of Bahá'u'lláh*. Translated by Shoghi Effendi. Wilmette, Illinois: Bahá'í Publishing Trust, 1952.

—— *Prayers and Meditations by Bahá'u'lláh*. Translated by Shoghi Effendi. Wilmette, Illinois: Bahá'í Publishing Trust, 1962.

Borgese, Elisabeth Mann, et.al. *A Constitution for the World*. Santa Barbara, California: Center for the Study of Democratic Institutions, 1965.

Clark, Grenville, and Sohn, Louis B. *World Peace through*

World Law. Cambridge, Massachusetts: Harvard University Press, 1960.

Constitution for the Federation of Earth. Lakewood, Colorado: World Constitution and Parliament Association, 1977.

Esslemont, J. *Bahá'u'lláh and the New Era*. Wilmette, Illinois: Bahá'í Publishing Trust, 1984.

Falk, Richard. *This Endangered Planet – Prospects and Proposals for Human Survival*. New York: Vintage Books, Random House, 1972.

Hainsworth, Philip. *Bahá'í Focus on Human Rights*. London: Bahá'í Publishing Trust, 1985.

Holy Bible, Revised Standard Version.

Hornby, Helen, compiler. *Lights of Guidance – A Bahá'í Reference File*. New Delhi, India: Bahá'í Publishing Trust, 1983.

Keys, Donald. *Earth at Omega – Passage to Planetization*. Boston, Massachusetts: Branden Press, 1982.

Lindsey, Hal. *The Late Great Planet Earth*. Grand Rapids, Michigan: Zondervan Publishing House, 1977.

Mendlovitz, Saul, ed. *On the Creation of a Just World Order – Preferred Worlds for the 1990's*. New York: Macmillan Publishing Co., 1975.

Mische, Gerald and Patricia. *Toward a Human World Order – Beyond the National Security Straitjacket*. New York: Paulist Press, 1977.

Myers, Norman, ed. *The Gaia Atlas of Planet Management*. London: Pan Books, 1985.

Nathan, Otto and Nordan, Heinz. *Einstein on Peace*. New York: Simon and Schuster, 1960.

Peace. Compiled by the Research Department of the Universal House of Justice, Bahá'í World Centre. Oakham, England: Bahá'í Publishing Trust, 1985.

Principles of Bahá'í Administration. London: Bahá'í Publishing Trust, 1973.

Rabbani, Rúhíyyih. *The Priceless Pearl*. London: Bahá'í Publishing Trust, 1969.

Bibliography

Reves, Emery. *The Anatomy of Peace*. New York and London: Harper and Brothers, 1945.

Riggs, Robert F. *The Apocalypse Unsealed*. New York: Philosophical Library, 1981.

Sanger, Clyde. *Safe and Sound – Disarmament and Development in the 1980's*. London: Zed Press, 1982.

Schell, Jonathan. *The Abolition*. New York: Picador, 1984.

—— *The Fate of the Earth*. New York: Avon Books, 1982.

Shoghi Effendi. *The Advent of Divine Justice*. Wilmette, Illinois: Bahá'í Publishing Trust, 1984.

—— *Citadel of Faith*. Wilmette, Illinois: Bahá'í Publishing Trust, 1970.

—— *Messages to the Bahá'í World 1950–1957*. Wilmette, Illinois: Bahá'í Publishing Trust, 1958.

—— *The Promised Day is Come*. Wilmette, Illinois: Bahá'í Publishing Trust, 1980.

—— *The World Order of Bahá'u'lláh*. Wilmette, Illinois: Bahá'í Publishing Trust, 1955.

Star of the West. 1910–1924. Reprinted in eight volumes at Oxford, England: George Ronald, 1978.

A Synopsis and Codification of the Laws and Ordinances of the Kitáb-i-Aqdas. Haifa: Bahá'í World Centre, 1973.

United Nations. *Program of Action*. 1978 Special Session of the General Assembly on Disarmament. New York: 1978.

Universal House of Justice. *The Promise of World Peace*. Haifa: Bahá'í World Centre, 1985.

Waging Peace. A compilation of the Writings of Bahá'u'lláh, 'Abdu'l-Bahá and Shoghi Effendi. Los Angeles, California: Kalimat Press, 1984.

NOTES AND REFERENCES

Introduction

1 *Synopsis*, citing Bahá'u'lláh p. 27.
2 'Abdu'l-Bahá, *Selections*, p. 32.
3 Shoghi Effendi, *Promised Day*, p. 123.
4 From a letter written on behalf of Shoghi Effendi on 16 Feb. 1932, *Peace*, p. 37.

I: From 'Disarmament' and 'World Poverty' to 'World Government'

1 'Abdu'l-Bahá, *Canada*, p. 50.
2 Clark and Sohn, *World Peace*, p. xv.
3 Reves, *Anatomy*, p. 210.
4 Schell, *Fate*, p. 226.
5 Nathan and Norden, *Einstein*, p. 339.
6 Schell, *Abolition*, p. 86.
7 Shoghi Effendi, *World Order*, pp. 40–41.
8 The proposals in Clark and Sohn, *World Peace through World Law* deal with these points in full detail.
9 United Nations, *Program*, paras. 110–11.
10 'Abdu'l-Bahá, *Selections*, p. 249.
11 Shoghi Effendi, *World Order*, p. 204.
12 Nathan and Norden, *Einstein*, p. 339.
13 Mendlovitz, *Creation*, p. 129.
14 See Paul Craig and Kenneth Watt, 'The Kondratieff Cycle and War – How Close is the Connection?', *The Futurist*, April 1985, pp. 25–7, for an exploration of the relationship between economic cycles and war/peace cycles.
15 See *Time* magazine, 11 Feb. 1985, p. 25 and 29 July 1985, pp. 38–43; and Schell, *Fate*, pp. 212–13.
16 Schell, *Fate*, pp. 209–10.
17 See also Falk, *Endangered*, pp. 257–9, for some historical perspectives on deterrence.
18 'Abdu'l-Bahá, *Secret*, p. 61.
19 Bahá'u'lláh, cited in Esslemont, *New Era*, p. 32.
20 Bahá'u'lláh, cited in Shoghi Effendi, *World Order*, p. 206.

21 Bahá'u'lláh, *Prayers and Meditations*, p. 295.
22 Mische, *Human World Order*, p. 61.
23 'Abdu'l-Bahá, *Selections*, pp. 31–2.

II: The World Government Debate

1 Schell, *Abolition*, pp. 15–19.
2 Myers, *Gaia*, p. 244.
3 Bahá'u'lláh, *Gleanings*, p. 253.
4 'Abdu'l-Bahá, cited in *Star of the West*, vol. V, no. 8, p. 115.
5 Myers, *Gaia*, p. 247.
6 *Ibid.*, p. 246.
7 Sanger, *Safe*, p. 15.
8 Bahá'u'lláh, cited in Esslemont, *New Era*, p. 40.
9 Shoghi Effendi, *Promised Day*, p. 122.
10 Universal House of Justice, *Promise*, p. 3.
11 Bahá'u'lláh, *Gleanings*, p. 260.
12 Shoghi Effendi, *World Order*, p. 202.
13 Fox, W. T. R., *The Absolute Weapon*, cited in Schell, *Abolition*, p. 39.
14 Mendlovitz, *On the Creation of a Just World Order* consists of articles by members of this project, an outline of which is provided in its introduction.
15 Shoghi Effendi, *World Order*, p. 45.
16 Mische, *Human World Order*, p. 288.
17 Keys, *Omega*, p. 43.
18 Green, Lucile W., in *Open Exchange*, Oct. – Dec. 1983, p. 33. It is interesting to note that the nations which lost the most in the last world war also seem to be the most conscious of the need to change the present nation-state system.
19 'Abdu'l-Bahá, *Secret*, p. 64.
20 Keys, *Omega*, pp. 16–17.
21 'Abdu'l-Bahá, *Secret*, pp. 66–7.
22 'Abdu'l-Bahá, cited in Shoghi Effendi, *World Order*, p. 37.
23 Keys, *Omega*, pp. 5–6.
24 Shoghi Effendi, *World Order*, pp. 41–2.
25 'Abdu'l-Bahá, *Promulgation*, p. 167.
26 'Abdu'l-Bahá, *Selections*, p. 306.
27 *Constitution* World Constitution and Parliament Association.
28 See 'Abdu'l-Bahá, *Selections*, pp. 306–7.
29 Shoghi Effendi, cited in Hornby, *Lights*, no. 636.

30 Schell, *Abolition*, p. 87.
31 See, for example, Shoghi Effendi, *World Order*, pp. 9–10, and Shoghi Effendi cited in *Principles*, pp. 44–5.
32 Bahá'u'lláh, *Gleanings*, p. 200.
33 Shoghi Effendi, *World Order*, p. 34.
34 Shoghi Effendi, *Promised Day*, p. 123.
35 See Lindsey, *Planet Earth*, chapter 8, and Anderson, *Coming Prince*, appendix 2.D.
36 The clearest proof of this is that both of the prophecies state that the period of this kingdom is to be '1260 days'. This period is sometimes given as 42 months (× 30 days per month = 1260) or as $3\frac{1}{2}$ years (= 42 months = 1260 days) or as $3\frac{1}{2}$ days, where days are counted as years, or as 'a time, two times and half a time' (= $3\frac{1}{2}$ half years = 1260 days). In the language of prophecy, 'days' are often counted as years, and thus this refers to a period of 1260 years. In addition to being found frequently in Biblical prophecies, this period is alluded to in the Qur'án and is specifically found in some of the Islamic 'traditions'. It signifies the Islamic dispensation, which ended in the year 1260 AH with the Declaration of the Báb. In the book of Revelation, the 'number of the beast' is said to be '666'. The first of the Caliphs appeared 666 years after the birth of Jesus, and the numerical value of his title is 666. These and many other fascinating proofs concerning the fulfillment of these prophecies are provided by 'Abdu'l-Bahá in *Some Answered Questions* and by Robert Riggs in *The Apocalypse Unsealed*.
37 Isaiah 2:4 (RSV).
38 Isaiah 9:6–7 (RSV).

III: Visions of the New World Order

1 Bahá'u'lláh, *Gleanings*, p. 249.
2 'Abdu'l-Bahá, *Secret*, pp. 64–5.
3 See 'Abdu'l-Bahá, *Selections*, pp. 306–7; *Star of the West*, vol. III, no. 17, pp.6–8.
4 Shoghi Effendi, *World Order*, pp. 203–4.
5 See 'Proposals for Charter Revision Submitted to the United Nations by the Bahá'í International Community', 1955.
6 *Ibid.*, p. 42, and 'Abdu'l Bahá, *Paris Talks*, pp. 88–9.
7 For general information on this topic see Hainsworth, *Human Rights*.

Notes and References

8 For a further discussion of some of the ramifications of these changes, see Clark and Sohn, *World Peace*, pp. xliv–vi.

IV: Getting There

1 'Abdu'l-Bahá, *Selections*, p. 297.
2 Mische, *Human World Order*, pp. 273–4.
3 The addresses of these organizations, and others, plus a brief description of each, may be found in the *Encyclopedia of Associations*, ed. Akey, pp. 1305–6.
4 For example, every day 40,000 children die from preventable diseases and malnutrition. Save the Children, *Annual Report*, 1984–1985, p. 6.
5 Universal House of Justice, *Promise*, p. 15.
6 *Ibid.*, p. 1.
7 The two chapters on strategies in Gerald and Patricia Mische's book *Toward a Human World Order* are a good example. (This book in general is an excellent analysis of the problems caused by the nation-state system and is well worth reading.) See also *On the Creation of a Just World Order*, edited by Saul Mendlovitz of the World Order Models Project.
8 Shoghi Effendi, *World Order*, pp. 45–6.
9 Shoghi Effendi, *Citadel*, p. 125.
10 *Ibid.*, p. 37.
11 'Abdu'l-Bahá, cited in Shoghi Effendi, *World Order*, p. 30.
12 'Abdu'l-Bahá, *Selections*, p. 307.
13 Bahá'u'lláh, cited in Shoghi Effendi, *Promised Day*, p. 5.
14 Schell, *Abolition*, p. 42.
15 Keys, *Omega*, p. 16.
16 Bahá'u'lláh, cited in *Promised Day*, p. 3.
17 Shoghi Effendi, *Messages*, p. 103.
18 Matt. 24:21–2 and 37–9 (RSV).
19 Shoghi Effendi, *Messages*, p. 104.
20 Shoghi Effendi, *Promised Day*, p. 4.
21 Bahá'u'lláh, *Gleanings*, pp. 342–3.
22 Shoghi Effendi, *Messages*, p. 103.
23 Bahá'u'lláh, *Gleanings*, p. 209.
24 Shoghi Effendi, *Citadel*, p. 126. The above sources encompass much of the Bahá'í teaching on this subject. Some additional sources include Bahá'u'lláh, *Gleanings* p. 118; Shoghi Effendi, *Promised Day*, pp. 1–3, 111–12, 122–3;

Shoghi Effendi, *World Order*, p. 193; Shoghi Effendi, letters written on behalf of Shoghi Effendi, and the Universal House of Justice, cited in Hornby, *Lights*, pp. 89–98; Rabbani, *Priceless Pearl*, pp. 189–95.

25 Matt. 5:5.
26 Mendlovitz, *Creation*, p. 119.
27 Falk, *Endangered Planet*, preface.
28 *Ibid.*, p. 3.
29 Schell, *Abolition*, p. 83.
30 Bahá'u'lláh, *Bahá'í Prayers*, p. 130.
31 Shoghi Effendi, *Promised Day*, p. 4.
32 Shoghi Effendi, *Advent*, p. 90.
33 Shoghi Effendi, cited in Rabbani, *Priceless Pearl*, p. 193.
34 Shoghi Effendi, *Citadel*, p. 38.
35 Universal House of Justice, cited in *Peace*, pp. 43–4.
36 Shoghi Effendi, *Citadel*, p. 128.
37 From a letter written on behalf of Shoghi Effendi, cited in Hornby, *Lights*, no. 278.
38 Bahá'u'lláh, cited in Shoghi Effendi, *Promised Day*, p. 116.

V: Conclusions

1 'Abdu'l-Bahá, cited in *Star of the West*, vol. VII, no. 15, p. 136.
2 Shoghi Effendi, *World Order*, p. 190.